SEEKING
Christ
THROUGH
Friendship

For where two or three are gathered in my name,
I am there among them.

—Matt 18:20

SEEKING
Christ
THROUGH
Friendship

JAN ALKIRE

Paulist Press
New York / Mahwah, NJ

Cover image by Anson0618/Shutterstock.com
Cover and book design by Lynn Else

Library of Congress Cataloging-in-Publication Data

Names: Alkire, Jan, author.
Title: Seeking Christ through friendship / Jan Alkire.
Description: New York : Paulist Press, 2019. | Includes bibliographical references.
Identifiers: LCCN 2019014269 (print) | LCCN 2019981206 (ebook) | ISBN 9780809154647 (pbk. : alk. paper) | ISBN 9781587688591 (ebook)
Subjects: LCSH: Friendship—Religious aspects—Catholic Church.
Classification: LCC BV4647.F7 A45 2019 (print) | LCC BV4647.F7 (ebook) | DDC 241/.6762—dc23
LC record available at https://lccn.loc.gov/2019014269
LC ebook record available at https://lccn.loc.gov/2019981206

ISBN 978-0-8091-5464-7 (paperback)
ISBN 978-1-58768-859-1 (e-book)

Published by Paulist Press
997 Macarthur Boulevard
Mahwah, New Jersey 07430
www.paulistpress.com

Printed and bound in the
United States of America

In memory of Leo Byron Thomas, OP

Praise the LORD!
Praise the LORD from the heavens;
    Praise him in the heights!

Kings of the earth and all peoples,
    princes and all rulers of the earth!
Young men and women alike,
    old and young together!

Let them praise the name of the LORD,
    for his name alone is exalted;
    his glory is above earth and heaven.

Psalm 148:1, 11–13

Spiritual Companionship: a friendship that includes Jesus as a third, very important friend.

Contents

CONTENTS

Acknowledgments

This book arose from an earlier program called "Formation for Spiritual Companions," offered by the Institute for Christian Ministries (ICM). Its teachings and wisdom came from ICM's founder, Leo Thomas, OP.

Father Leo had a dream: Empower laypeople to bring Christ's healing love to a hurting world. Help them discover their God-given gifts and deepen their relationship with the Lord. Show them how to support one another in their work and in their personal life. I owe an inexpressible debt of gratitude to Father Leo for passing on his dream to me so that I could pass it on to others.

I am indebted to the two spiritual directors I've had: the late Father Jack Murphy, SJ, and Sister Joyce Cox, BVM. What a blessing to have had such wise guides on my spiritual journey!

Three people walked many extra miles with me by reading every word in this book and giving me feedback: Sister Joyce Cox, Joan Bell, and Candy Stickney. Thank you, ladies, for your labor of love! Thanks also to the diverse, zesty, affirming group of writers in north Seattle: the Write Night folks. Those Thursday classes kept me motivated—one thousand words a week.

Then there were the invisible people—all the faith-filled men and women who prayed for me as I wrote this book.

Where would I be without them? Their commitment and prayers gave me strength.

Finally, I am profoundly grateful for the spiritual companions I've had throughout the years, some for only a brief time, some for decades: Margaret, Barbara, Candy, Joan, Sue, Sharon, Dinny, Kathleen, and Pat.

Spirit of the Living God, thank you for each of these holy people. Thank you for their presence in my life, along with their prayers and their shared work to bring your love and peace to others. Amen.

Introduction

YOUR LIFE
A SACRED JOURNEY

Your life is a sacred journey.
It is about change, growth, discovery, movement
    and transformation.
It is continuously expanding your vision of what is
    possible,
stretching your soul, teaching you to see clearly
    and deeply,
helping you to listen to your intuition.[1]

The Nativity Church in Arbanasi, Bulgaria, fooled me because its exterior looked like an old, abandoned barn. Our tour guide had described the church in glowing terms, even going so far as to call it "the Sistine Chapel of the Balkans." But as our bus arrived at the grey, low-slung building with shuttered windows, I muttered to myself, "We've come all the way for this?"

Grumpiness turned to awe as I stepped inside and stared, slack-jawed, at the thousands of frescoes and murals that cover the ceilings, walls, and beams of this spectacular church.

Bible scenes invite visitors to ponder our holy and not-so-holy Judeo-Christian history. Other scenes contain mortality messages.

The mortality message that intrigued me the most was a mural in the form of a clock. Called the "Wheel of Life," it starts with our birth at 6:00 a.m. From there we climb ever higher through youth, reach our physical/mental peak at noon (indicated by a crown on a seated figure), then begin to decline. By the time we arrive back at 6:00—our death—we're as helpless as the day we were born.

The Wheel of Life poses a question to viewers: Do you accept this journey, or do you deny it? Today we're awash in messages that lure us toward the latter: This skin treatment will make you look twenty-five again. This pill gives fast pain relief. This seminar will change your life. And now, through the miracle of modern living, it's possible to subtract twenty years from your current age: sixty is the new forty. Stop the clock. Avoid all suffering. Cancel all aging. You can live forever.

Well no, of course we can't. But it's easy to believe the hype. If we do, we'll live lives of constant frustration and eventual desperation when reality intrudes: the accident, the divorce, the unemployment, the illness, the loss of vigor that comes with aging. Even sadder, a warped focus can cause us to overlook sacred moments in real life: a sunrise, a caring note, a child's drawing, a friendship, a word of encouragement from God.

If we expend our energy trying to freeze-frame and control life at its zenith, we'll miss the real life God has in mind for us. We'll miss joy and fulfillment and so much more. What a loss. But this need not happen. Instead, God invites us to a sacred journey of change, growth, discovery, and transformation.

Sacred journeys do not happen alone. To have the abundant life that Jesus said he came to bring us,[2] we need companions.

Introduction

We need fellow travelers to walk with us as part of our relationship with God.

This book shows how to share your spiritual life with companions. It offers tools to strengthen your gifts of listening, encouragement, and support. And it includes reflection ideas for you to explore. I pray it helps you expand your awareness of the amazing grace that lies within you and all around you.

Jan Alkire, 2019
Seattle, Washington
www.JanAlkire.com

PART I
Journeys

CHAPTER 1

Journeying with Spiritual Companions

IN THIS CHAPTER:

Story: From carpooling to spiritual companionship

Scripture examples of people who walk with others

What we hunger for

The value of spiritual companions

Faithful friends are a sturdy shelter: whoever finds one has found a treasure.

—Sirach 6:14

In the 1980s, a woman named Meg[1] and I began carpooling to healing ministry training sessions in Tacoma, Washington. We weren't friends. We simply were acquaintances looking for a practical way to get from point A to point B. Ride sharing meant we could use express lanes and also save money on fuel.

During those 60-mile round-trip drives, we chatted about everything and anything. The world, our nation, our city, our churches: we covered it all. Eventually we started talking about personal matters, including our families, our joys, and our struggles. As trust grew, we became friends.

When the ministry training sessions in Tacoma ended, Meg and I decided to be a prayer team, praying with hurting people who were seeking healing. After each session, we would spend a few minutes praying for one another's needs. We entered into the unknown waters of spiritual companionship before we had a name for it or knew what it was. Our journey was unique but not original. We walked in the footsteps of what others have done throughout human history.

WALKING WITH OTHERS

The first words God speaks in the Genesis 2 Creation story are, "It is not good that the man should be alone" (2:18a). Thus began countless stories of people in the Bible who, like Meg and me, walked with others:

Moses. He argues with God that he can't possibly confront Pharaoh: "O my Lord, please send someone else!" (Exod 4:13), and agrees to lead the Exodus only after God promises the aid of his siblings, Aaron and Miriam. I have motivated, capable brothers and sisters, but even if God solemnly promised me their aid, I may have balked and echoed Moses's request that he send someone else.

The seventy-two whom Jesus sent out two by two. He sent them together for support and shared ministry (Luke 10:1–20). Meg and I sensed the same sending-forth at the end of our training and the start of becoming a prayer team. Ministering together has yielded more fruit than what either of us could have accomplished alone. We discovered that one plus one equals far more than two.

Paul and numerous companions—especially Luke, who sailed with Paul, got shipwrecked with him (Acts 27:6–44), and wrote a history of the earliest followers of Christ (Acts of the Apostles). There was much drama, including some conflict. Many shared lives. As of the time of this writing, I have never ended up needing to abandon ship. Still, a spiritual journey is not an easy one. It can, and usually does, involve the pain of self-discovery. It also can, and often does, involve the realness of Paul's relationships.

Most of the people we read about in scripture made heroic sacrifices. Many covered great distances. Others stayed in one location. All had one thing in common: They weren't alone. They were joined by others in a journey of body, mind, and spirit.

Our own journey may not be as physically perilous as those in the Bible, but we need others because life itself includes struggles, risks, and, perhaps, worse, a daily tyranny of the urgent. Text messaging, schedules, traffic, and people's demands press in on us. The cacophony can drown out the voice of our inner being until it becomes impossible to nurture or even recognize our deepest hungers.

WHAT WE HUNGER FOR

Hunger for the Sacred

Each fall, a glossy catalog from an upscale shopping mall arrives in the mail. Its cover features a svelte model and one word: "Be." The message is clear: Shopping is the essence of your being, of who you are as a person. Buy our stuff. It will make you happy.

The secular world does meet needs, such as our need for food and shelter. Things go awry when the house or car or smartphone or career or whatever becomes a substitute for the sacred. Something's missing, but what is it?

Hunger for Experiences of God

I attended Sunday school as a child. I learned the Ten Commandments and tried to obey them. I memorized prayers. Until my mid-thirties, I knew about God in the same way I knew about Abraham Lincoln—nothing personal because I had never met them. Therefore, I wasn't aware of either one having an impact on my personal life. I ran on my own strength and willpower. My knowledge of God was good, but deep down I also hungered for a relationship—for experiences of God and God's love for me.

Hunger for Spiritual Growth

Because we are living beings, at any one point in time we're either spiritually growing or wilting, learning or getting set in our ways, moving forward or backward. But a rut is so... comfortable. We may long for growth but fear what that might bring.

Hunger for Health and Healing

Everyone I've ever met wants physical, emotional, relational, and spiritual wholeness. But there's always some pain in our life isn't there? When the healing we seek eludes us, loneliness can arise as well, a feeling of isolation from all those seemingly healthy, carefree people out there.

Hunger for Spiritual Companions

Many people go to church on Sundays, pray the prayers, sing the hymns, shake the pastor's hand afterward, say hello to acquaintances, then return home without any in-depth conversations being possible.

We need communities in general and faith communities in particular. They ground us. They give us a sense of how the world "works." They teach us moral values and cultural perspectives, as well as attitudes about life, relationships, and God. Without communities, we would perish.[2]

These larger communities are essential, but they cannot know individuals at a soul level. This is where one-on-one friendships and the gift of spiritual companions come in.

THE VALUE OF SPIRITUAL COMPANIONS

I have several spiritual companions and have been blessed by them in innumerable ways. Here's what I've discovered and what others have told me:

1. *A spiritual companion helps us see our experiences through eyes of faith.*

   I have a spiritual director, and I've had counseling, but this isn't either of those, where someone offers me wisdom and help and I receive it. Instead, spiritual companions are friends who love God and walk side-by-side with the Lord and with one another. It's a friendship that consciously includes God as a third, very important friend.

   My companion and I get together for lunch and share what's happening in each of our lives and how

7

we sense—or don't sense—God's presence in those events. We pray together for each other's needs. In between get-togethers, I can phone her to wail that what I'm trying to write *isn't working.* I can text message to ask for prayers for an upcoming trip. And because this is a relationship of equals, my spiritual companion does likewise. She might wonder if God notices the struggles she and her husband are having to find a new home. She can email me with an update on a son's job search, knowing I've been praying for him and care about the outcome. In other words, we do what close friends tend to do: support and share with one another, but with the added element of including God in the relationship.

2. *Sharing with someone moves experiences outside the confines of the mind.*

Wisdom from a bumper sticker: "Don't believe everything you think." Alone, the human brain can wing off into weird directions. Persistent thoughts may cycle through the mind like an unwelcome song. A few that sometimes plague me:

Worry, such as health concerns, where a tiny symptom must be a terminal illness. How long do you have to live? How much agony will you endure as you die? (Note: Sometimes called "catastrophizing," worry is one of my specialties. Give me a topic—any topic— and I can turn it into a tragedy. I'm the queen of mental melodrama.)

Anger. That pastor's sermon really bugged you. His theology is so off base. Just thinking about it makes you boil. But even if all is bliss in your personal life, one glance at the nightly news or the Internet can give rise to a storm of anger. Congress! Crime! The economy!

Despair, including hand-wringing about the state of the world. Why try, when everything is so rotten? Talk shows and naysayers can fuel thoughts that leave no room for hope and the goodness of life itself.

Paranoia. A coworker's irritability must mean she hates you. Maybe she's after your job. This type of thinking presumes an ability to read minds, a skill set I have yet to master (though I occasionally try).

Expressing troubling thoughts out loud helps us discover what we're thinking about God, our life, and our experiences. Good listeners enable us to see reality more clearly, even if they hardly say a thing. We gain a wider perspective. Like fog lifting from a pond, situations become clearer.

3. *A spiritual companion helps us stay focused on God's unique call to us.*

    It's easy to get distracted from the uniqueness of our own journey. There are so many choices and so many needs in the world, in our family, and within our faith community. How do we sort out our choices? How do we maintain the ability to hear the voice of our shepherd?

    In religious circles, questions like these fall into a category called "discernment." Experts devote entire careers to studying, writing, and speaking about it. Chapter 12 in this book gives an overview of discernment and how it relates to spiritual companionship. Here I'll simply say that a companion primarily helps us discern God's call not by giving advice, but rather by being a sounding board—easy to say, hard to do.

4. *A spiritual companion offers us encouragement and support.*

    When our world is stormy and feels out of control, a spiritual companion offers a safe harbor to rest and receive nourishment, a brief reprieve from the external and internal storms of life. After getting together with a companion, I usually feel less alone and more at peace. Feelings like these lead to an awareness of a fifth benefit of spiritual companionship—one of the best ones for me.

5. *Through the acceptance of a spiritual companion we come to know God as being loving and safe. We grow in trust of God as we grow in trust of our companion.*

In the next chapter, we'll explore this fifth item: our relationship with God. But first, here are a few possibilities for reflection on this chapter.

FOR YOUR REFLECTION

1. Spiritual companionship is a friendship that consciously includes God as a third, very important friend. You may already have someone like that in your life—a peer relationship that has a spiritual component. Who comes to mind? Recognizing this gift that you already have can help you and your companion(s) develop the relationship more intentionally.

2. This chapter describes several human longings. How many do you identify with? Which one is upmost in your mind at this time (hunger for the sacred; for deep experiences of God; for spiritual growth; for health and healing; for spiritual companions)?

3. Sharing moves experiences outside the confines of the mind. Do you ever struggle with thoughts that go on and on? Four possibilities are mentioned in this chapter: worry; anger; despair; paranoia. (You may

have others as well.) If any of these are an issue for you, how do you deal with them?

Closing Thoughts from Others

"It takes a lot of courage to show your dreams to someone else." (Erma Bombeck)

"Dig deep into any human being and you will find something divine." (Saint Augustine)

CHAPTER 2

Journeying with God

IN THIS CHAPTER:

Choosing a road: smooth or rocky? With Jesus or without?

How beliefs impact our relationship with God

Question: What do you want Jesus to do for you?

Two features in any relationship with God: one internal, one external

The importance of spiritual companions in a relationship with God

Christ comes into each of our lives today if we remain open to the possibility. After all, Jesus has the long view and knows the road ahead. Onward! Incredible things lie ahead.

—Sister Julia Upton, *Give Us This Day*

Decades ago I had a prayer experience where, in my mind's eye, I saw two pictures simultaneously, like a split-screen picture on TV. One was a sunny rose garden with a level path winding through groomed flower beds. Each rose was in full, brilliant bloom in what looked like a twentieth-century Garden of Eden. Weeds had apparently not yet been invented.

The other picture was a mountain landscape above the timberline. It featured drizzle, rocks, scrawny plants, and a steep, rocky path that disappeared into greyness beyond a trailhead. It also featured Jesus standing at the trailhead, inviting me to choose which path I wanted.

Never before or since have I had such an awareness of the gift of free will. Wow, did I love the look of that rose garden and the beauty of its perfection. But that's not where Jesus was; so, reluctantly, I chose the rocky path.

When I told my husband of my decision, I said, "Can you believe I chose that path?"

"Of course," he said. "You'd be crazy not to choose it. Where does the rose garden path lead?" I didn't know. "Where does the path with Jesus end up?" That was easy—heaven. (Note: My husband was an agnostic at the time. He didn't believe in God, but as a Boeing analyst who helped airlines project future growth, he knew the importance of looking ahead!)

My particular path with Jesus has indeed had its rocky moments, including an illness that plagued me on and off for twenty-eight years. When the illness was "on," I'd sometimes host a pity party for myself. Then the words of an old song would come to mind: "I beg your pardon; I never promised you a rose garden." "Very funny," I'd say to Jesus, while at the same time admitting that I freely chose the rocky path, not the rose garden.

WHAT DO WE BELIEVE?

That rocky path prayer experience has helped me stay grounded in reality. It's helped me clarify what I expect from God. It's also given me an awareness of what others believe and how that impacts their relationship with God.

- *"I've never been angry with God, and I never will be."* A friend said this. She believed anger at God was the unforgivable sin Jesus warned us about. She later confided that on the day her father had a massive stroke, she felt a surge of anger at God. Was she damned? I told her I hoped not, because I certainly have angry moments with God.

  My friend thought God was always looking for her to trip up, yet she came from a religious tradition that teaches once saved, always saved. This clashed with her competing belief that God would send her to hell if she ever had a negative feeling about him.

- *"God took my husband a year ago and now he's given me cancer."* An old woman told me this before going into surgery. I hear it often in my work in healing ministry, usually stated as, "My illness is God's will."

  Here's how a spiritual director once described it: "Imagine God loves you with an infinite love. One day he says, 'I love this person so much, what can I give him? I know—rheumatoid arthritis!' Or 'MS!' Or 'cancer!'"

  In this belief, God has a sadistic way of showing love—if, in fact, he does love us. I told the woman that God doesn't give people cancer, that he was present with us in the hospital room. Then, I asked her if she would like me to pray with her for a few minutes—for God to be the divine physician guiding the surgeon's hands. She liked that idea and so we prayed.

- *"I don't want to have anything to do with a god who allows natural disasters."* This came from a man after an earthquake in Afghanistan caused chaos and death. Belief in an all-powerful, all-loving God clashes with the reality of suffering. A Savior who deserves the title should be able to—and want to—shelter the innocent from sorrow and pain.

  I told the man I had no answers. I said I have a list of questions I want answered when I meet God face-to-face in the next life. This question tops the list. Until then, I just try my best to relieve suffering whenever and wherever I encounter it.

Any relationship with God brings us face-to-face with mystery. We cannot fathom the depths and wisdom and love of the great I Am. We can only say yes or no to the journey. And if the journey has already begun, ours is the freedom to say yes or no to deepening the relationship. Moments of decision often occur during a major life transition—an illness, divorce, or job loss, the move to a new city or birth of a child.

In *Healing Ministry: A Practical Guide*, Father Leo Thomas described two major transitions he experienced simultaneously in 1948. He had fought on the front lines in World War II and now was fighting a different battle: a severe case of PTSD. He also was trying to decide whether or not to become a priest.[1] Clarity came during a retreat when the leader invited everyone to meditate on a passage from the Gospel of Mark: the healing of a blind beggar (10:46–52).

A man named Bartimaeus is begging at the side of a road. He's blind at a time when disabilities were believed to be a sign of God's displeasure and punishment for sin. Hearing that a holy man named Jesus is passing by, he calls out, "Jesus, Son of David, have mercy on me!" The crowd tells him to be quiet, but he keeps shouting for mercy.

Jesus stops and invites the beggar to come to him. Bartimaeus throws aside his cloak and approaches Jesus, who asks, "What do you want me to do for you?"

Bartimaeus responds, "My teacher, let me see again." Jesus restores his sight, and Bartimaeus follows him on the way, healed physically and, probably, spiritually and emotionally as well.

"WHAT DO YOU WANT ME TO DO FOR YOU?"

During Father Leo's 1948 retreat, God asked him the same question Jesus had asked Bartimaeus two thousand years earlier. It led to what he said was "a profound, ever-deepening vision of the truth....It comforted me and helped me discern that God was calling me to become a priest. Its effect on me has persisted throughout my adult life."

Now God addresses the same question to each of us: "What do you want me to do for you?" In Bartimaeus's case, the answer seemed obvious. What did Jesus expect him to say—"Heal my back"? Why ask when the answer was so obvious? Here's one reason offered by James Martin in *Jesus: A Pilgrimage*:

> Jesus sees something liberating in identifying and naming our desires. Once we scrape off any surface selfishness, our deepest longings and holy desires are uncovered: the desire for friendship, the desire for love, the desire for meaningful work, and often the desire for healing. Ultimately, of course, our deepest longing is for God. And it is God who places these desires within us. This is one way God calls us to himself. We desire God because God desires us.[2]

16

God does desire our friendship, our love. But a relationship with God is risky. How do we enter into it? Personally, I'm not a dive-in-instantly type of person, whether it's a relationship or a body of water. I want some assurance that what I'm entering into is safe. So most of my decisions occur step-by-step, which brings to mind my experiences with labyrinths.

STEP-BY-STEP

A labyrinth is like a maze with no blind alleys or dead ends. It has one path to the center and back out. You enter at the perimeter, then slowly, slowly walk toward the center. One of Christendom's most famous labyrinths is in the Gothic cathedral in Chartres, France. The forty-two-foot-wide design in its stone floor has attracted masses of pilgrims since its completion in the 1200s. I've walked its replica in the Episcopal cathedral in San Francisco. I've also walked an outdoor one at a retreat center in Oregon—challenging because it was springtime and the path had not been mowed since the previous fall!

Just when you think you've almost arrived at the center of a labyrinth, the path takes you closer to the perimeter again—so much like life itself and so much like our spiritual journey. When we finally do reach the center of our being, we encounter not only our deepest self but also the One who says, "Remember, I am with you always, to the end of the age." (Matt 28:20b)

Labyrinths illustrate two features in any journey with God, one exterior, the other interior. The exterior piece is physical and obvious: *We show up.* We show up in a faith community, we show up by praying, we show up by serving God. By our actions, we say to God, "You are important to me. Therefore, I'm going to spend time with you and for you, even when I'm not in the mood."

The interior piece of our journey with God is less obvious: being open to God. We make this decision daily. But what if God is a tyrant? Or what if God is an ineffective weakling? Worse yet, what if God causes all manner of disasters and illnesses?

Wounded beliefs like these may shut the door on any relationship with God. At best, we might leave the door slightly ajar and peek through a spiritual crack, doing just enough to appease this Mysterious One whom we do not understand and cannot control. Move forward in this relationship? Change? Grow? No way. Not possible. Unless....

Unless our journey with God includes others. Here is where spiritual companions enter in. In addition to the benefits mentioned in chapter 1, they can be instruments of healing spiritual wounds. Their presence can give us the courage to enter more deeply into a journey with no guarantees. We are not alone. Someone walks beside us. Therefore, together we can say yes to God's invitation to trust in him. This is the One who says to each of us,

> I know the plans I have for you...plans for your welfare and not for harm, to give you a future with hope. Then when you call upon me and come and pray to me, I will hear you. When you search for me, you will find me." (Jer 29:11–13a)

FOR YOUR REFLECTION

1. Perceptions have the power to wound or to heal. This is especially true for ones that are barely recognized, or not recognized at all. One way to deepen your

self-awareness about your perceptions of God is to reflect on how you respond to highs and lows that occur in life. What, *if any*, are your thoughts and/or feelings about God when the following occurs?

a. A baby comes into the world whole and beautiful.

b. A baby is born with a serious birth defect.

c. The beauty of a flaming, multicolored sunset takes away your breath.

d. A terrorist sets off a bomb in a theater, killing many innocent people.

e. A family reunion is stressful and a reminder of past grievances.

f. A family reunion is filled with joy, laughter, and love. (Note: family reunions often are a combination of items "e" and "f"!)

g. Music in a church service makes your spirit soar.

2. Meditating on scripture can reveal surprising things about God and about ourselves. Try it with the passage about the healing of the blind beggar (Mark 10:46–52). Read through the story a couple of times, imagining that *you* are Bartimaeus.

a. You are saying, "Jesus, have mercy on me!"

b. Jesus stops and invites you to come a bit closer.

c. You come closer.

d. Then he says, "What do you want me to do for you?"

e. What is your answer? What do you want Jesus to do for you at this particular time?

3. One essential in any journey with God: showing up.

a. Do you belong to a faith community and worship with them often? If yes, is that life-giving for you? If not, what options do you have?

b. Are you able to spend time alone with God on a regular basis? If yes, when and where? If not, what obstacles are blocking you?

c. In what ways are you serving God at this time? Within the family? Through your career? Through your faith community?
4. Have you ever thought about your relationship with God as a journey? How great a risk would it be to move forward from where you are now?

Closing Prayer

God of all creation, I ask for the grace to journey with you, to move forward with your Son, to grow. Show me the way. Amen.

PART II
Companionship Essentials

CHAPTER 3

Beginnings

SEEKING AND FINDING

IN THIS CHAPTER:

Why seek a spiritual companion?

Spiritual direction

Finding spiritual companions

Clarifying expectations

Hazards in the relationship

Blessings of spiritual companionship

> Search, and you will find; knock, and the door will
> be opened for you.
>
> —Matthew 7:7b

Jesus tells us we'll find if we search—including finding spiritual
companions. This assumes we want companions, and since

one of my mottos in life is "never assume anything," perhaps this is a good place to ask a basic question: Why seek spiritual companions? Chapter 1 described several reasons:

hunger for the sacred

hunger for experiences of God

hunger for spiritual growth

hunger for health and healing

hunger for support in our work, family life, and
    decision-making

These reasons may make the desirability of spiritual companions seem obvious. But any relationship is risky, even a relationship with God. It takes courage and faith to seek when we don't know the outcome. So here's a question: Do you want to try this? If so, let's first look at what spiritual companionship isn't: spiritual direction.

SPIRITUAL DIRECTION

Once upon a time, spiritual directors...directed. Saint Thérèse of Lisieux wrote *Story of a Soul* because her director/prioress ordered her to do so. Saint Teresa of Avila wrote her autobiography for the same reason. Centuries passed, bringing with it an awareness that adult seekers don't need parent figures telling them what to do. Instead, they need the wisdom of experienced guides to help them grow and discern God's presence in their lives.

Recognizing my own need for growth, in 1979 I asked a Jesuit priest named Father Jack Murphy if he'd be my spiritual director. He said yes, even though he had not yet had any director training. So, we met. We sat and looked at each other. I wondered what I

Beginnings

should say, and he apparently wondered the same thing about his role. Finally, I started talking about prayer because it was, after all, spiritual. He responded with wisdom and affirmation.

Thus went many of those first sessions: I talked about my prayer life and Father Jack responded. Eventually, however, it became obvious that both of us were bored. I mean, how long can you focus exclusively on a twenty-minute period of time in a day before there's not a whole lot more to say? Then, one day I happened to mention an experience of God I'd had outside of my prayer time. The session suddenly came to life. The Lord was with me every moment of my day, and I began to look for that reality and share it with Father Jack. He was wise and, instinctively, an excellent spiritual director.

Father Jack later received specialized training for spiritual directors.[1] As with all directors, his relationship with me was the vertical one of a mentor, not the horizontal one of friendship. Faith sharing focused on my journey, not his. I didn't phone him to chat as I do with friends. Instead, we made appointments and met in his office.

Father Jack was my director for thirty years. I now have one who, like him, blesses my life with encouragement, wisdom, and support. I am grateful for these holy people who have mentored me through times of turbulence and discernment. Each is a joy to be with, a gift from God.

I think all serious seekers of God could benefit from having both a spiritual director and spiritual companions. But good, qualified directors are often hard to find. That makes it especially crucial to find life-giving companions.[2]

FINDING SPIRITUAL COMPANIONS

As noted earlier, spiritual companions are friends who include Jesus as a third, very important friend. We find them the way we find any friends, but with an added component: potential companions are in relationship with the Lord and want to deepen it by journeying with others. Often they meet through a shared activity that evolves into a shared spiritual journey. That's how Meg and I met and became companions (described in chapter 1).

Another option: meet through a program that helps seekers find others and learn how to journey together. That's what happened to two men who attended the same church but had never met. Van and Burt each felt spiritually alone and wanted to deepen their relationship with God but didn't know how until they responded to an invitation to attend a Cursillo retreat in their area.

For three days, fifteen men worshiped together, heard talks, met in small groups, shared their faith with one another. At the end of the retreat, everyone was encouraged to support each other's journey by continuing to meet in small groups. Van, Burt, and several other men decided to do this on Saturday mornings at a coffee house. To date, they've been meeting for ten years.

When I look at Christians, including ones in my parish, I know if we weren't brothers and sisters in the Lord, our paths would rarely cross: PhDs, blue-collar workers, retirees, new parents, religious liberals and conservatives—we're good people who sometimes have little in common.

Occasionally, however, I "click" with someone like Meg, someone older or younger than I, the same or different denomination, married or single. These are not the relevant factors. What counts are traits such as these:

spiritual maturity

mutual interests and goals

an ability to listen

a kind, nonjudgmental spirit

love and acceptance of me, warts and all

an ability to maintain confidentiality (discussed in
chapter 4)

Put these traits together, then add one more essential for this relationship to work: time. It must be possible to meet on a fairly regular basis.

The above knowledge can help us find a companion who's a match. To heighten our ability to recognize someone we already know—or meet a new person—I recommend prayer. The Spirit knows all possibilities for our future, a future that can include other seekers, one that God assures us is always full of hope.[3]

CLARIFYING EXPECTATIONS

When Meg and I first decided to be companions, we were clueless. We wanted to try this but what did it mean? What did each of us want? Part of the success of our relationship came through addressing these questions and discussing how we could meet each other's needs. In short, we clarified our expectations.

As unique individuals, each of us enters into relationships with a set of expectations based on past experiences. Often we're only dimly aware of them; sometimes we're oblivious to them. They then take on the quality of "you must meet my expectations." This causes stress and confusion, even in the best relationships. For example:

1. Bride to new husband: "You think I should make a lunch to take to work with me every day? I always buy mine. It's not that expensive."

2. Hostess: "I said dinner would be at 6:00 and Gail isn't here yet. She thinks being late is no big deal and expects us to wait, but the food is getting cold."
3. Employee: "My boss emails me at 9:00 p.m. and thinks I should answer it right away. I have a family, a life! I'm not on call 24/7."

In my own life, painful experience reinforces my "never assume anything" motto. When I remember and act on it, it lowers my level of stress because I have a realistic idea of what to expect of myself, of other people, and of situations.

Looking at your situation, if you openly discuss how each of you envisions your sessions, it will lessen confusion and enable the two of you to reach an agreement that meets the needs of both of you. Items to clarify include the following:

- What each of you hopes to achieve in the relationship.
- Agreeing on confidentiality: What you share stays within the four walls of where you meet. It doesn't get passed on to anyone.
- How often you'd like to meet.
- A location and time that will work for both of you. (This can be a difficult item to work out. Resist getting discouraged.)
- Expectations for your relationship between sessions, including frequency of contact that would be acceptable for each of you.
- What kind of activity you envision taking place during your get-togethers.

Meg's and my sessions gradually became a pattern that works for us:

- Beforehand, we schedule when we can meet without distractions, allowing one and a half hours so we won't be rushed.
- We meet at either Meg's house or mine, bringing our own lunches.
- We turn off our phones.
- While eating, we catch up on what's going on in our personal lives—for instance, a job stress, an upcoming trip, news about a child or grandchild, a situation at church, a health issue. It would be easy to get sidetracked with impersonal topics such as sports or politics, so we've agreed to stay away from subjects like that.
- Our lunch conversations often segue into what comes afterward: prayer. We start with a focus on God's presence with us, then move into praying for one another's needs. This is covered in chapter 10: "Praying with/for a Spiritual Companion." Here I will simply say our goal during prayer is to experience God meeting us in our needs—no advice giving, just listening and praying.
- At the end, we spend a few minutes debriefing what has occurred during our session. (Debriefing is covered in chapter 7: "Endings.")
- Before parting, we schedule a time to meet again—for us, once a month.

At the end of a session, I usually feel more peaceful, more aware of God's presence. Between sessions, Meg and I sometimes phone each other if a particular need for prayer arises, such as an illness, a decision to make, a family crisis. Her prayer support lifts me up, strengthens me, helps me remain clearheaded.

Meg's and my sessions evolved over time. In the case of Van and Burt, their Cursillo group meetings have more structure.

They take turns responding to the following three topics recommended by Cursillo. Knowing the focus ahead of time helps everyone recognize and reflect on experiences shortly after they occur.

1. *Prayer*: This can mean something in a companion's spiritual life, perhaps an experience of God he's had, or his struggles to fit prayer into a busy schedule. The goal is to nurture each person's relationship with God.
2. *Study*: This can mean learning more about God, the spiritual journey, human nature, etcetera. Usually this comes from something a participant has read or heard and then reflected on. Study helps participants develop gifts and talents that God can then use to do good in the world.
3. *Action*: This may be as simple as carrying out an elderly neighbor's trash, or as time-consuming as tutoring a child with a learning disability. In addition to benefitting those they assist, putting faith into action benefits companions because the opposite pattern— receiving without giving back—eventually leads to being as spiritually dried up as Death Valley.[4]

Those are two descriptions of spiritual companion sessions. Undoubtedly there are more, but I believe the key elements in all of them are

- regular get-togethers,
- freedom from distractions when meeting, and
- shared prayer in order to focus on the most important Person in this relationship: Jesus.

One other item: In my experience, women and men usually share differently and focus on different things. This is one reason I recommend that women have female companions and men have male ones. Take, for instance, the couple who decided to each write about their fifty years of marriage. The husband's memoir focused on his job and struggles to support a large family. The wife wrote about giving birth to seven children and raising them to adulthood. One marriage, two journeys that sure looked different for the husband than for the wife. He needed male companions. She needed women.

Today's two-income households often look different than this couple's. Still, men who share their journey with other men tell me their focus tends to be on career issues and concerns about their future. As for women, I've noticed that we (including myself) tend to put our emotional and spiritual energy into relationships: for instance, family members, friends, or people at work.

HAZARDS IN THE SPIRITUAL COMPANION RELATIONSHIP

Every relationship carries with it a risk of harm, of causing hurt or of being hurt, of things ending badly. Spiritual companionship is no exception, especially because of the level of closeness it can reach. It brings to mind an experience I once had while watching an air show.

The Navy's Blue Angels roar into Seattle each summer and dazzle us with a spectacular performance. Six planes fly wingtip to wingtip in perfect unity. They do barrel rolls, they fly sideways, upside down, and right side up. They rocket skyward then fan out like petals of a flower opening up. After each aerobatic feat, they regroup for another maneuver that leaves everyone gasping in awe and, yes, a bit of fear.

Usually the show occurs south of our home. One year, however, it took place a mile east of us and the planes regrouped directly over our house—very loud, very close, and so low that the evergreen trees in our yard rustled as they flew over. They came in from different directions, but by the time they left our backyard, they were together, six planes flying as one.

For some reason, each time I saw the regrouping I felt an irresistible urge to pray a prayer of praise. This distressed me. "What are you doing?" I asked myself. "Why are you praying? Are you worshiping these guys?" My efforts to resist praying failed, so along about the fourth time the planes approached, I asked God what was going on. Why was my spirit so drawn into prayer?

What came to me was that the unity I was seeing in those six planes was, in a way, an analogy for the Trinity: three persons, one God, each unique yet totally united. Relationships such as spiritual companionship can mirror this oneness. They can live out the words of Jesus when he prayed, "I pray that they may all be one. Father! May they be in us, just as you are in me and I am in you" (John 17:21, GNT).

Jesus is describing a relationship that takes us into the mystery of the Trinity. He is talking about the kind of union that exists between God the Father and God the Son: "May they be in us *just as* you are in me and I am in you." That is God's longing for each of us: that we become profoundly one in the Lord. Spiritual companions have an opportunity to experience this kind of unity at a felt level. What a gift.

And what a risk. As the above thoughts about the Trinity came to me, I felt myself shrinking back, avoiding the invitation to such closeness with others. Blue Angel planes occasionally crash. So do relationships. Tragedies can happen and that's why it's good to be aware of where things can go awry.

The most common hazard: a spiritual companion relationship can start to take precedence over all other ones. For example:

32

You've found a soul mate—someone who listens to you and accepts you just as you are. No one in your family is interested in your spiritual journey. They may not even be interested in God. Why spend time with them? Why invest yourself in those relationships? And why spend so much volunteer time with people in your church? They don't appreciate your efforts. They gripe about everything. Besides, a lot of members don't seem like very good Christians anyway.

If you ever find yourself thinking thoughts like these, resist them. Recognize them for what they are: temptations. They are temptations to skew your priorities away from loved ones, friends, and the wider community. They are temptations to become too exclusive with another person, too emotionally possessive of that person's time and energy.

Sometimes—especially with someone of the opposite sex—there may be temptations to behave in sexually inappropriate ways with a companion. That's what happened to two Christians whose choices destroyed their marriages and wounded their faith community. And that's why, to lower that risk, I recommend that companions be the same gender: women with women, men with men. Whatever the combination, good emotional and physical boundaries are essential.

Another hazard: companions can lose sight of their priorities. *Loved ones take precedence over a spiritual companion.* Time spent with a companion is a gift, not an obligation. So, for instance, if Tom's son has a basketball game scheduled at the same time that his companion Bill wants to meet, Bill will need to work out a time that doesn't conflict with Tom's parental responsibilities. Why? Because there is a duty of love that comes with whatever state of life you and I have chosen. Spiritual companions do not interfere with commitments. Our goal is peaceful union without a claim on each other's life.

BLESSINGS OF SPIRITUAL COMPANIONSHIP

An old radio show called *A Prairie Home Companion* often transitioned between acts with fake ads. One ad was for Powder Milk Biscuits: They "give shy folks the strength to get up and do what needs to be done." It ended with exuberant singing: "Has your family tried 'em, Powder Milk? (*Powder Milk!*) Has your family tried 'em...."

Fantasy biscuits aren't about to give anyone the strength to get up and do anything. Relationships, however, can. That's one of the blessings I've experienced through spiritual companionship: it makes me stronger, more capable of becoming the person God is calling me to be—less crabby, more patient; less blind, more aware of others; less me, more you.

Spiritual companionship is meant to bring life to all our relationships. That's one way to discern its health: Are we growing in love for family, friends, faith community, and others in our life? Are we drawing closer to them?

A strong companion relationship also helps sustain us in a career and other activities. Annoyances become less annoying. Fears become less fearful. For instance, after Meg and I meet, talk, and pray together, I feel strengthened to keep on writing, more confident about the work I'm doing for God.

The best blessing of all? Grace that comes to me through my spiritual companion heightens my awareness of the loving presence of the risen Lord, my primary source of strength. This is the One who invites each of us to join him on a grand adventure. We may be like Peter who fell at Jesus's knees and begged him to go away after he hauled in a massive catch of fish (Luke 5:8). Our reluctance to say yes to Jesus may be like Peter's: an awareness of the sullied state of our soul. Or it may be fear of stepping into new, uncharted territory, or concern about the disapproval of loved ones.

Reasons to say no abound, but Jesus's invitation remains. It doesn't keep him from reaching out to each of us to say, "Follow me. I love you. I have plans for your life." A companion can help calm our fears and give us the courage to say yes.

FOR YOUR REFLECTION

1. Do you already have a spiritual companion (with or without naming the relationship as such)? If so:
   a. What traits mentioned in this chapter do you see in him/her?
   b. Has this relationship helped you grow in love for family, friends, faith community, and others in your life?
2. Do you currently have a spiritual director/mentor/advisor?
   a. If not, do you have an interest in finding one? Where might you look?
   b. If you do have a spiritual director, what is the relationship like?
   c. If you have both a director and a companion, how do these relationships differ? How are they similar?
3. Regarding expectations: If you already have a spiritual companion, what are your sessions like? Have you clarified your expectations of each other? If you do not yet have a companion, how do you envision this kind of relationship and your role in it?
4. Looking at the relationship hazards covered in this chapter: Are any of them familiar to you from personal

experience or the experiences of others? Are you willing to risk this kind of life-giving closeness?

5. Finally, I invite you to reflect on this scripture passage: "Search, and you will find; knock, and the door will be opened for you" (Matt 7:7). What, or whom, are you seeking? What, if anything, have you found?

CHAPTER 4

Confidentiality

A BASIC BUILDING BLOCK

IN THIS CHAPTER:

Story: Betrayal of a confidence

Confidentiality: a basic building block in spiritual companionship

Confidentiality: an act of love

Maintaining confidentiality

> Have you heard something? Let it die with you. Be brave, it will not make you burst!
>
> —Sirach 19:10

Julie met Amy at a women's group in their church. They both had a zest for exercise, so once a week they walked together around Seattle's Green Lake. As they walked, they talked.

Mostly Amy spoke of her life and personal struggles while Julie listened and offered words of encouragement.

The walks and chats lasted until the day Julie decided to share a recurring nightmare about a past mistake. Within a week, everyone in the women's group knew what she had said—and done. Waves of anger washed over Julie: anger at Amy but also at herself for sharing something so personal, for being so *stupid*. Then came feelings of embarrassment. Acquaintances knew something about her that was private. Did they see her differently now? Were they talking about her? What could she do?

Julie ended her walks with Amy and limited future chats with her to topics like the weather. But Amy's betrayal of a confidence wounded Julie deeply. She dropped out of the women's group and became guarded about creating other friendships. Could she trust anyone? Better not take the risk.

CONFIDENTIALITY: A BASIC BUILDING BLOCK IN SPIRITUAL COMPANIONSHIP

Chapter 3 ("Beginnings") looked at essentials in a spiritual companion relationship. Beneath each of these essentials lies trust, including trust that what I share with my companion will be held as sacred, as confidential. Therefore this chapter will look at confidentiality as a basic building block for a spiritual companion relationship.

Perhaps this word brings to mind signing HIPAA regulation papers giving so-and-so permission to share medical and/ or legal information with somebody or other. These are professional situations. But confidentiality also extends into the realm of human relationships. It is a specific way to handle information we receive from another person—a way of receiving information and then dealing with it in a loving way. I don't know how Amy received Julie's information. She certainly failed in how she dealt with it afterward.

CONFIDENTIALITY: AN ACT OF LOVE

Love recognizes, respects, and safeguards the boundaries between two people. When receiving information from someone, love considers whether that information is public or private. Love asks a question before sharing someone's personal information: *Do I have this person's permission to tell this to others?* Without specific permission, what I've heard is confidential.

In our society, people sometimes disregard the boundaries of others and use information as a source of power. If I know something about you, I am "in the know." I am part of an inner circle of power. I have the power to use that knowledge to impress others. This is one reason people gossip. If what I know about you is something you would rather other people not know—such as the fact that you are having employment problems—I also have the power to hurt you by damaging your reputation.

Today, people sometimes use information as a source of entertainment. I can view something you tell me as being like a living drama, a reality TV show that you are part of. An event in your life can feel like going to the movies. A tragic movie, a romantic one, a comedy. It's all so titillating, so exciting. Then, afterward, I naturally want to go out and tell others what a great "movie" I just saw—your movie, an event in your life.

Confidentiality doesn't use information as a source of power or entertainment. Instead, it regards personal information as something that belongs only to that person and to God. When you share something with me, it doesn't become my information. *It still is yours.* Your self-disclosure is a sacred treasure that remains with you.

Confidentiality is also a sacred trust. If you tell me something personal about yourself, you are trusting me to care for it very, very carefully. Without your explicit permission I am not free to share it with others. Not my spouse or my friends or my pastor—not anyone. Through active listening and empathy, I share your burden with you. I do not share it with others.

Confidentiality says when you tell me about a struggle or conflict, I will not think less of you as a person. I will still treat you as Jesus would treat you: as a beloved child of God. So if you tell me about, say, a parenting problem, I will not begin to look upon you as a failure. Rather, I will do my best to see you as someone engaged in a spiritual journey that only God can fully understand.

MAINTAINING CONFIDENTIALITY

"Three can keep a secret if two of them are dead." So said Benjamin Franklin, long before personal news could go viral in nanoseconds. His words and the Internet notwithstanding, spiritual companions can maintain confidentiality. For me, the easiest way to do this is to treat everything that occurs during a session as sacred. It stays in the room where my companion and I have met (a spin on "whatever happens in Vegas, stays in Vegas").

But what if you have a concern about a companion's safety or the safety of others? This would be rare and has never happened to me. But if someone ever seems to be in danger of hurting him- or herself or others, a moral responsibility will lie before us: a responsibility to act.

Example: Your companion is clinically depressed and talks about suicide as "a way out." If you think he might harm himself soon, call 911. If the danger doesn't seem immediate, seek professional help *and tell your companion what you're going to do.* He may hate you for doing this, but contacting a physician, counselor, or EMT in a crisis situation does not violate a confidentiality agreement. It is an act of love.

The above scenario would be highly unusual. Keep in mind that an emergency in any aspect of life calls for outside help. The norm in spiritual companionship isn't an emergency.

Confidentiality bears rich fruit because it builds trust, a crucial component in any close relationship and one that is all too easy to violate. Ask God for the grace to maintain confidentiality, to treat your companion's sharing as holy ground on which the two of you stand.

FOR YOUR REFLECTION

Confidentiality is difficult to ponder because it naturally gives rise to memories of someone violating our trust and regrets about our violating someone else's. This reflection takes a look at those two probabilities.

1. Have you ever conveyed someone's information to others, information that you now realize was confidential?
   a. If yes, who was this person? What was the event?
   b. If the mistake harmed the relationship, has it been possible to repair the damage?

    c. Much wisdom in life comes from reflecting on past mistakes. Did you learn anything from what happened? If so, what?

    d. Everything in this chapter applies to the future, from today forward. Resist the temptation to condemn yourself for any past error. Treat yourself with love and forgiveness. To do this, I suggest turning to God in prayer. One scripture passage: "Do not remember the former things, or consider the things of old. I am about to do a new thing; now it springs forth, do you not perceive it?" (Isa 43:18–19a)

2. Has someone ever violated a confidence you entrusted to him/her?

    a. If yes, what did you confide?

    b. What was the result of this person telling others what you said? Did your relationship suffer? If so, in what way?

    c. With or without ever again confiding in this person, are you able to forgive their breach of confidentiality? This may be hard to do! If so, I suggest turning to God for help. Ponder scriptures about God's mercy and love. One idea: Matthew 6:9–13 (Lord's prayer); also Luke 11:2–4.[1]

Closing Prayer

God of mercy, give me your gifts of mercy and forgiveness— forgiveness of myself and of others for any breaches of confidentiality. Help me set aside the past so I have the freedom to focus on the future. And from this day forward, help me maintain confidentiality whenever it is needed. Amen.

CHAPTER 5

Listening

A DIVINE ACTIVITY

IN THIS CHAPTER:

Story: Job and I

Basic types of conversation

Listening essentials

Listening to God

Qualities of effective listening

Four nonlistening stances

Listening and spiritual companions

> Listening is a magnetic and strange thing, a creative
> force. The friends who listen to us are the ones we
> move toward, and we want to sit in their radius.
> When we are listened to, it creates us, makes us
> unfold and expand.
>
> —Karl Menninger, MD

As mentioned in chapter 2, I once had an on-again, off-again illness that lasted twenty-eight years. Initially, no matter how much I ate, I lost a pound a week. After six months, I was twenty-five pounds underweight. I ran the numbers. In another six months I'd be fifty pounds underweight. And probably dead. When doctors failed to discover what was wrong, I turned in desperation to the only one who did know: God. Thus began a relationship that has blessed me, challenged me, and surprised me beyond anything I ever expected.

During flare-ups of my illness, I learned a lot about listening, mostly because few people did it well. Sometimes I felt like a biblical Job, who was alone amidst friends with plenty of words but no clue what he was going through. How could they know? They weren't listening.

What may seem easy is actually hard, energy-draining work. It's one of the essentials in any relationship: family, professional, neighbor, acquaintance, spiritual companion. Everyone—even God—longs to be heard. How can we do that well? That is the focus of this chapter.

BASIC TYPES OF CONVERSATION

Conversations differ. Who is this person? Why are the two of you talking? How much time do you have? Knowing these things can help clarify what's appropriate for this conversation with this person. That, in turn, strengthens the relationship.

Ideally there's a back-and-forth rhythm in most interactions. Lunching with a friend, sharing ideas with a coworker, chatting with a grocery store cashier, talking with a loved one on the phone: You talk while they listen, then they talk while you listen. A certain equality exists.

Occasionally, however, a conversation moves deeper. Perhaps

you run into a neighbor and ask him how he is; he says he's just been diagnosed with cancer. When something like this happens to me, I can feel a mental shift as my focus changes to a total listening mode. I'm now engaged in an in-depth conversation where my task is to listen to this person with both mind and heart. Several listening essentials can pave the way for that to occur.

LISTENING ESSENTIALS

1. *Establish mutual trust.*

   If I distrust you, my mind and heart will probably be closed to anything you say. I will feel guarded or withdrawn. I may be physically present but emotionally absent. Likewise, if you distrust me, anything you tell me will probably be superficial.

2. *Relinquish the need to be heard.*

   When I'm really listening to you, I give up my need to respond. My only responses will be brief (such as "oh," or "I see") or nonverbal (such as nodding my head). I'm not saying anything other than letting you know I'm listening. I resist the urge to tell my own story—a strong tendency if you say something that triggers a memory in my own life. ("Wow, the same thing happened to me a few years ago....")

   When struggling with a temptation to speak instead of listen, a couple of questions may help:

   Where is the focus of attention right now? When I'm the listener, the focus shouldn't be on me.

   If this is a stage, where is the spotlight at this moment? It belongs on the actor, not the audience. I don't get up on stage and start adding my own material.

SEEKING *Christ* THROUGH *Friendship*

Another technique to help stay focused: Some Native Americans have a tribal "talking stick," where the person holding the stick is the only one who can talk. When we're in the role of listener, we might picture an imaginary "talking stick" or pencil or whatever. Who has the floor now?

3. *Give up expectations of what the other person will say, do, or be.*

For the moment, during the time I'm listening to you, I give up what I think you should say, do, or be. This can be tough if you express strong emotions such as anger, or if you say things I disagree with. But it isn't my job to change you or convert you. My role is to emotionally and spiritually walk beside you and listen openly to what you tell me. In situations where some sort of help might be appropriate, understanding should come first. Without that, whatever assistance I offer will likely be pat answers or answers based on my situation, not yours.

4. *Be at peace.*

Anxiety is a barrier to effective listening. Listening to your points of view about God and about life can scare me. What you say might change me in ways that take me out of my comfort zone. Whenever that happens, all I can hear is the sound of my own inner turmoil and my own thoughts.

LISTENING TO GOD

I try to use the above essentials when listening deeply to someone. I also intentionally shift into a spiritual space and try to focus on God and God's love for that person, to hear the way God hears.

When we're in a spiritual space, we listen to the one who is speaking with us, but we also listen to God. This requires an attitude of faith. It is not a technique. It is a divine activity. When we listen to people in this way, they may experience being listened to not only by us but also by God. It can be a life-giving, transforming experience.

Our role model here is the risen Lord walking with two disciples on the road to Emmaus (Luke 24:13–35). The first thing he did when he appeared to them was ask what they had been talking about. He listened to their answers and heartache before he said or did anything else.

Spiritual listening is a primary activity of spiritual companions when they meet for a session. They might have social conversations between get-togethers if their lives cross paths elsewhere, but when meeting as companions, they listen to each other *and* God as they converse. This is holy listening. This is journeying together as fellow pilgrims.

PERSONAL QUALITIES NEEDED FOR IN-DEPTH LISTENING

Imagine this: You're pouring out your heart to a person who's frowning at you, has crossed arms, and occasionally says, "tsk, tsk." OK, that's hard to imagine because you probably wouldn't bare your soul to someone who should only be dealing with inanimate objects. What we need when seeking a listener is a person who is loving, genuine, and compassionate.

Love

I used to bring communion to Catholic patients in a hospital when the chaplain had a day off. Some patients were dying, some were getting ready for surgery, many were grieving, many were scared, a few were angry at God or at me.

When I recall that ministry and think of love, one patient comes to mind. She had schizophrenia, and that made me nervous. How was she going to behave? The woman also had false teeth, and as she opened her mouth to receive communion, the teeth started to fall out. No big deal, but for some reason this repulsed me. I closed my eyes and prayed, "Lord, if you don't show me something right now, I'm going to have to leave this room." Immediately I sensed Jesus saying to me, "Just as you did it to one of the least of these who are members of my family, you did it to me" (Matt 25:40). A change swept over me—a love from God for this woman. I stayed. She received communion, after which I said a prayer with her for healing and peace.

Love like this is a nonpossessive warmth, an *agape* love like what God has for us, even amid our imperfections and illnesses. God calls us to convey this love to others without expecting them to earn it by talking or acting in a certain way. It isn't cozy feelings we naturally have for puppies and babies. Instead, *it is a gift from God*, a gift that's essential when we're in the role of listener.

Genuineness

I once visited a hospitalized friend who had a serious infection. When I arrived, Liz was lying in bed clutching a rosary. She looked relieved to see me, and when I asked what was going on, she told me her doctor said she wasn't responding to any medications. She might die.

"Oh, no!" I gasped. "How are you doing with this?"

"I'm scared," she said. "Especially in the middle of the night. All I could do last night was lie here in the dark with my rosary.

I don't even know how to pray the rosary, but just holding it made me feel a bit better."

We chatted like this for a while—Liz talking, me responding—two friends in a back-and-forth conversation with the focus staying on Liz. I did my best to emotionally stay with her, and after about fifteen minutes she said, "You know, this is totally different from a visit I had this morning from a chaplain. She asked how I was, then while I talked she sat there staring at me. Didn't say a word. After a while I felt like saying, 'Gee, lady, why don't you just leave a tape recorder here. I'll talk into that.' It felt weird."

The chaplain's visit floundered because only one person was present: Liz. The chaplain withheld who she was. She was as blank as a wall and talking to a wall does feel weird. Whenever I encounter someone like this, I tend to speak faster and faster, more and more until pretty soon I'm the one who's weird. Nothing good comes from that kind of conversation.

Genuineness means I am myself with someone. I'm not a phony. Nor do I withhold who I am. I'm not a blank. That is our challenge when we are listeners: to be fully present to someone, keeping the focus on that person and, at the same time, still being ourselves—genuine.

Compassion

Look up the word *compassion* in a dictionary and the first synonym that pops up probably will be *pity*. Pity looks at someone in a gutter with an "I'm glad I'm not him" attitude. Compassion emotionally gets in the gutter with him. Pity looks down on someone from on high. Compassion is an emotion of equals where we sense what it is like to be *this* person in *this* situation.

Compassion hurts. The word literally means "suffer with." When we walk in another's shoes for a while, we do suffer with that person. Few are willing to do this.

FOUR TYPES OF NONLISTENING

If we're paying attention to other people, their pain and needs naturally give rise to a desire to say something helpful. But first we must listen closely, deeply, and lovingly. If we don't do that, we'll almost certainly come forth with a slew of unhelpful listening responses, such as the following four.

I. Distancing

In his book *Turn My Mourning into Dancing*, Father Henri Nouwen recalled visiting a widow whose home had just been wrecked by a hurricane. Staring at the devastation, she said her life had become meaningless. She was a burden to everyone. "There is only one thing left for me to do," she said. "To die."

This would have been an ideal time for Nouwen to recall Paul's words to the Romans. "Rejoice with those who rejoice, weep with those who weep" (Rom 12:15). But no. Instead, he said, "You have no reason to be depressed. Look—you have children who love you and like to visit you. You have charming grandchildren...." A litany of reasons to be happy ended with this clincher: "Besides, few people in this neighborhood fared as well as you in the storm."

Father Nouwen later regretted his response to this woman's grief. He wrote, "I did not help her with these words....I had not accepted her feelings, but instantly fought her in a competition of arguments. When I left, I went from a woman feeling more sad than before, more burdened because I had not even acknowledged I had heard her."[1]

Father Nouwen made a classic distancing mistake: instead of joining this woman in her pain, he tried to talk her out of it. He said when we do this, we "act out of our need to stand back from the discomfort we fear we might feel. We secretly, restlessly want to move from the place where it hurts. Our evasions do not help others, of course, but rather cause them to put up defenses and drive away those who need someone to care."

During my years with a chronic illness, I heard plenty of distancing statements. Some were clichés: "Count your blessings". Others sounded soothing: "Oh, you poor dear." Many tried to sound encouraging:

- "You look great!" (I didn't. I sometimes looked like roadkill.)
- "It'll get better over time." (What the heck did they know?)
- "Everything will be all right." (A global statement signifying nothing.)

This third item was—and still is—the most maddening for me because things sometimes don't turn out well. A loved one dies. An illness worsens. An addict continues on a downward spiral. So now when someone says that everything will be all right, I say, "Really? Did God tell you that?" "Uh, no."

People who distance themselves think they're being helpful and usually go away feeling good, believing they have succeeded. That's also true for the next type of unhelpful responding.

2. Unsolicited Advice-Giving

Scene 1: A woman at a conference sees me bypass the conference lunch and microwave my own special-diet food. She tells me microwaving destroys all nutrients in food. I should stop microwaving my food.

Scene 2: After making a pie worthy of a trash can, I seek out a former roommate whose pies bring on swoons of ecstasy.

She walks me, step-by-step, through the process of creating flaky pie crusts worthy of requests for more.

Advice is helpful when we seek it, when we recognize a need (perhaps, edible pies) and are open to learning. The flood of how-to books and articles in today's market shows that positive advice is not only needed but also welcomed.

Trouble arises when advice is offered without our requesting it. The woman at the conference adopted a superior stance and presumed she knew more than I did about technology and about my needs. She left me feeling disheartened. It was hard enough to have a special diet. Now I'd been told I should give up one of my tools for coping with it.

Unsolicited advice is especially unhelpful when it occurs in response to something someone shares. This can come across in moralizing tones, where "should" often appears, a word that always makes my guard go up.

Personally, I think the expression "the patience of Job" comes from his tolerance of several of literature's most annoying moralizers. Job's so-called friends blame him for the tsunami of disasters that have overwhelmed him. They say God inflicted this suffering on Job because of his sins. He should "fess up and repent." "If you direct your heart rightly, you will stretch out your hands toward him....Surely then you will lift up your face without blemish; you will be secure, and will not fear" (Job 11:13, 15). Does this help? Of course not. Moralizing tends to make people feel guilty or resistant or hostile toward the advice-giver. It doesn't change lives.

Unsolicited advice can also be expressed in a manner that my father liked to call "bossy wossy"—heavy on commands, short on love and compassion: "Stop feeling sorry for yourself! Get out there and look for a new job. This one is no good for you."

Why do people offer us unsolicited advice? Why do *we* sometimes do this? For one thing, people are born to help, and helping naturally creates warm feelings within us. We're good; we're competent; we're helpers. Another possibility: We may care about others but get sidetracked with a desire to control, instruct, or reform them. Even when a piece of advice is offered oh so subtly, people know. They know they're being talked down to; they know we think they're too weak to handle something without our help. With that awareness comes a raising of defenses and a lessening of chances that they'll share more of themselves with us in the future.

3. Competing

Roy tells his friend Max that his boss is making his life miserable—demanding that he work overtime without pay, criticizing what he does, blaming him when things go wrong. Max responds, "Man, I know just what you mean. My boss is driving me nuts too. Let me tell you the latest...." With that, Roy's issues fade into the background as the spotlight turns onto Max and his problems. He may think this is a form of empathy, a way to let Roy know he understands his problem. Instead, his response means he's no longer the listener; he's the speaker.

Competing can rise to lofty levels of nonlistening in group gatherings such as cocktail parties and reunions. You tell a joke. Before the laughter even dies out, someone else tells another one that tops yours. Or as you share a memory during a reunion, others keep adding asides to what you're saying, taking the spotlight off of you and putting it onto themselves.

Whatever form it takes, competing violates a listening essential mentioned earlier in this chapter: relinquishing the need to be heard. It's an easy mistake to make, especially if people believe their response tells you they identify with your problem. They assume their experience matches yours. But you are a unique child of God with a unique life. Nonlistening presumes otherwise.

4. Absence

The scene: a table in the dining area of a cruise ship en route from Hawaii to San Diego. It's breakfast and the husband is looking at a magazine. His wife is attempting to converse with him.

The conversation: None. Comments by the wife are greeted by silence or a grunt. Finally she says, "Do you like the way my hair looks today?" Still reading, he grunts an apparent yes, at which point she sweetly says, "Dear, in order to answer that question you have to look at me."

Watching this vignette unfold, I wanted to turn to this woman and suggest that, contrary to what her eyes could see, her husband was absent. It's a classic form of nonlistening, but today's ever-smarter cell phones have raised the problem to pandemic levels:

- A couple sits in an elegant restaurant, not gazing into each other's eyes but, instead, looking at their phones.
- A mother with toddlers in a stroller doesn't talk to them as she walks. Precious time with her children is lost while she checks her phone for messages.
- Several students walk side by side across a college campus, all of them text messaging someone somewhere else, oblivious to everything except the tiny screen in front of them. If one of the students vanished into a sinkhole, the others wouldn't notice.[2]

In each of the above examples, *people aren't where they are.* They're in a mental space that doesn't require their physical or emotional presence, a "virtual reality" that creates the illusion of closeness without actual human contact. Pope Francis comments on this growing trend in *The Joy of the Gospel*:

> Some people want their interpersonal relationships provided by sophisticated equipment, by screens and systems which can be turned on and off on command. Meanwhile, the Gospel tells us constantly to run the risk of a face-to-face encounter with others, with their physical presence which challenges us, with their pain and their pleas, with their joy which infects us in our close and continuous interactions.[3]

People who live via their phones may sincerely believe they're also present to their surroundings, including to you. Perhaps that belief explains popular behavior in today's society: multitasking.

Everyone multitasks, for example, gardening while listening to a ball game, eating lunch while chatting with friends. Trouble arises when people think it's possible to be fully, mentally present in two places at once: Do math homework and watch TV; check phone messages and drive; send out a text message and listen deeply to you. If you object, they may say, "I'm listening," and repeat your last sentence. ("Uncle Zeke is sick.") That's not listening. That's echoing.

Multitasking is tempting because our lives are busy, and it feels like it's possible to mentally focus on more than one thing at a time. Neuroscientists disagree. They have shown that when we multitask, we rapidly shift our attention from one task to the other—from TV to homework then back to TV, from cell phone to driving then back to cell phone, from phone screen to a person next to them. No depth can be achieved when this occurs, no profound ideas, no deep relationships.

The behavior continues because the belief persists that we can be in two places at once. It brings to mind a TV segment I once saw: Researchers selected some test subjects who firmly believed in their ability to simultaneously drive safely and do other things. They took the people to a track, put cameras in their car, had them drive the course without distractions, then go through it again while doing different tasks: eat a sandwich, count backward by sevens, alphabetize some CD titles, talk on the phone, etcetera.

Without distractions, the drivers aced the course. With distractions the second time around, they toppled orange cones, ran stop signs, veered off the road, collided with fake cars and a fake deer. One woman crashed into the deer then immediately said, "That didn't happen."—this while the cardboard animal was protruding from the grill of her car.

Cell phones have made multitasking possible anytime, almost anywhere. At their best, they convey information and enable us to get in touch with others when needed. But if someone's phone consumes hours in their day, it robs many people, not just the user, of the closeness and depth of face-to-face relationships. Listening becomes impossible. It doesn't even begin.

LISTENING AND SPIRITUAL COMPANIONS

So far, the points covered in this chapter apply to relationships in general. Here are a few points to keep in mind when meeting as spiritual companions.

- About those pesky phones: Writer Anne Lamott once said the only good reason to have a phone at the dinner table is if you're waiting to hear from a hospital that an organ donor has been found for you. What's true for the dinner table also holds true for spiritual companions while meeting. Phones don't belong. They need to be turned off, not just silenced. If that isn't possible because one of you is, perhaps, on call at work, then this is not the right time to meet. Reschedule the session for a time when both of you can be fully present, totally focused on one another and on God.

- Expect it to take a number of sessions for you and your companion to establish the kind of rapport needed in this relationship. It takes time to build trust and develop a rhythm of listening and sharing with one another.

- As spiritual companions, neither of you is superior to the other. You are equals—sisters or brothers in the Lord—walking alongside each other. At a practical level, this means equal listening time, equal time for sharing.

- While your companion shares what's on his mind, your role is to join him in that space and listen deeply, keeping the focus on him. This isn't about you. This is about your companion. Then the two of you switch roles and your companion becomes the listener while you share what's happening in your life, perhaps where you sense, or don't sense, God in a situation.

- When you're the listener, expect to want to offer advice. Resist it! Instead, help your companion tell his story and explore feelings. Provide support, encouragement, and affirmation. (Affirmation, an essential ingredient in spiritual companionship, is covered in the next chapter.)

CONCLUSION

Listening is a great gift that spiritual companions give one another, but it's not easy. In *The Road Less Traveled*, Scott

Peck, MD, says, "When we love another we give him or her our attention; we attend to that person's growth....Listening well is an exercise of attention and, by necessity, hard work. It is because they do not realize this or because they are not willing to do the work that most people do not listen well."[4]

Listening *is* hard work. I encourage you to pray for a willingness to engage in this labor of love. Pray for God's grace to be an attentive listener.

FOR YOUR REFLECTION

Becoming a good listener is a goal of this chapter, which covers a number of challenging issues. If you have any relationships with anyone, you have at least occasionally made listening mistakes in the past. And you probably know people who span the spectrum of listening abilities, from grades A to F. Using your life experiences, I invite you to reflect on the following questions.

1. Looking at each of the four listening essentials (establish mutual trust; relinquish the need to be heard; give up expectations of what the other person will say, do, or be; be at peace):
   a. Do you know someone who comes close to embodying these essentials? Who? How does it feel to be with this person?
   b. Which of these essentials is most difficult for you? Why?
   c. When listening deeply to someone, have you ever experienced shifting into a spiritual space where

you include God and God's love for that person—where you try to sense God's presence with you as you listen? If so, what was that experience like?

2. Looking at personal qualities needed for in-depth listening (love; genuineness; compassion):
   a. What one thing did you learn from this section—one takeaway?
   b. What do you do when you encounter someone who is hard to love? (Avoidance is a natural response, a road I have often taken.) If you have ever asked for God's grace to love this person, did anything change?

3. Looking at four nonlistening responses (distancing; unsolicited advice-giving; competing; absence):
   a. How do you feel when someone doesn't listen to you? Which of these responses annoys you the most?
   b. Which of these responses is the most tempting for you when you're the listener?

4. Psalm 139:1, 4–6

O LORD, you have searched me and known me....
Even before a word is on my tongue,
   O LORD, you know it completely.
You hem me in, behind and before,
   and lay your hand upon me.
Such knowledge is too wonderful for me;
   it is so high that I cannot attain it.

The Psalmist here writes as one who has a one-on-one relationship with God, who listens and cares about him/her. Do you believe God listens to you? If so, how do you experience it? What are some of the ways God answers you? When and how do you listen to God?

5. Scott Peck says listening is hard work. What have you learned from this chapter that will enable you to embrace this difficult work more effectively?

Closing Prayer

God of love, thank you for the people who listen to me. I ask for whatever gifts I need to listen to others as you listen to them: with love, acceptance, and understanding. Amen.

CHAPTER 6

Affirmation

A WAY OF LIFE

IN THIS CHAPTER:

Affirmation vs. criticism

What affirmation is and is not

Discounting

Four ways to affirm others

Obstacles to affirmation

Affirmation: a way of life

> Encourage one another and build up each other, as indeed you are doing.
>
> —1 Thessalonians 5:11

When I was a physical therapist, the main questions with each patient were "What is the problem?" and "How do we fix it?" "What's wrong with the way this man is walking?" "What exercises will help this woman's range of motion?" Questions like these led to healing and a better quality of life for many.

Today, our society continues to discover flaws as a way to deal with issues. Trouble arises when character and ability are seen as problems to be solved. "What's wrong with this person?" "What criticisms will help him improve his character and his work?" It brings to mind a long-ago story about two writers' clubs at the University of Wisconsin: "Stranglers" and "Wranglers."

Participants in both clubs held great promise for future success, but they adopted opposite styles of critiquing one another: The all-male Stranglers tore into each other's work with complete honesty and no sensitivity to feelings. Meanwhile, the all-women Wranglers looked for the positive in every piece, supporting and affirming one another in their efforts.

The result: The critical Stranglers produced no writers of note, whereas from the affirming Wranglers came several well-known authors, including Marjorie Rawlings, Pulitzer Prize-winning author of *The Yearling*. Without affirmation, the Stranglers wilted while the Wranglers blossomed.

WHAT AFFIRMATION IS AND IS NOT

One way to describe affirmation is to first look at what it isn't:

- It isn't the "power of positive thinking" or phrases taped to a mirror, such as "I am special." That's a generic statement, not an affirmation.
- Affirmation is not flattery or mechanically recited kind words. Someone's "Have a nice day," followed by my

"You too" do not touch the core of anyone's life. They are social niceties that say little about either person.

- Affirmation isn't manipulation to get something from someone.
- It isn't the same as a compliment, wonderful as those are. For instance, if I compliment you on your dessert, I'm talking about your food, not you.

Affirmation reveals to people the good we see in them. It is a statement of truth, where *we see someone as God sees that person*. That may not always be easy: the teenager pouting at the dinner table because she can't use the car tonight; the minister whose sermons bore me to death; the loud neighbor with the trashy yard. In cases like these, God doesn't always cross my mind. I don't want to see these troublesome people as God sees them. I want what I want, and what I want is for them to change.

This attitude isn't going to transform anyone's life, including my own. So eventually I try to turn my heart and mind to God. I pray for God's love for the person who irritates or puzzles me. I pray for grace, rather than just my own limited insights. I also pray for a willingness to see what *is* rather than what is not, because God always sees with eyes of love.

That's the first step in affirmation: seeing people as God sees them—seeing the goodness that God created in them. Then comes a second step: *we allow ourselves to be moved by the goodness we see*. This means going beyond our intellect and being touched by what God shows us. That teenager is pouting about the car at the moment, but every day she shows kindness and patience to her younger brothers. The minister who gives lousy sermons is doing his best to be faithful to God in an area where he may have been poorly trained. As for that messy neighbor? That may need a bit more prayer for God's insights and love.

Now comes the third step in affirmation: *we show people their goodness, their giftedness*. We do this in a way that makes it real to them. Our insights won't do much good if we stop short of letting someone know what we see. Because people aren't mind readers, they don't know how God has gifted them and loves them if nobody shows them these things.

The teenager, the pastor, the neighbor: how can they be affirmed? Often with difficulty, especially when they're being selfish or cantankerous or obnoxious. In those cases, instead of affirmation, I'm tempted to engage in discounting.

DISCOUNTING

I grew up in a neighborhood with lots of kids. We ran, biked, sledded, fought, played games, climbed trees, built things, fell down, got up, and played some more. All except a gangly boy named Billy with buck teeth who had raw, chapped skin under his lower lip because he kept running his top teeth over that area. He desperately wanted to play with us but we wouldn't let him. Instead, we teased him, egged him on, taunted him. It pains me to think of my participation in this group cruelty. I pray that Billy found a way to recover from our merciless behavior, which was a classic case of discounting.

Discounting is the opposite of affirmation. It's different than talking behind someone's back, which, of course, is harmful. Discounting diminishes people's self-worth *to their face*. It minimizes them by tearing them down or putting them down. That's what our little mob of kids did to Billy on a regular basis: again and again, we put him down.

Discounting is pervasive, and perhaps as old as humanity itself. If there's anyone who hasn't been on the giving or receiving end of this behavior, I've yet to meet that person. We are created in the image and likeness of God. Discounting distorts this truth and misuses the power of language.

Language is like a coin with two sides: use and misuse. I can use words to build up or tear down, to love or shred, to criticize or support—in short, to affirm or discount. One day, after telling my spiritual director about my unfortunate skill with sarcasm, he said the only way to rid myself of this negative use of words would be to reject the positive as well. Was I willing to give up the gift? Well, no. So instead of tossing out the good with the bad, I entered the struggle to tame this verbal power. It hasn't been easy because sometimes discounting comes more readily to mind than affirmation.

Discounting often carries one of two messages: "You're not one of us," or "You're deficient. Something's wrong with you." Classic forms include the following:

- Demeaning nicknames and labels such as "klutz" that put people into a prison of someone else's making.
- Jokes: ethnic, gay, racial, blond, put-downs about men or age, and, yes, lawyer jokes (Dick the Butcher in Shakespeare's *Henry VI, Part 2*: "The first thing we do, let's kill all the lawyers").
- Backhanded compliments: "Hey, we arrived safely with you at the wheel. It's a miracle!" Or parents telling their daughter, "You look good when we finally see you in a dress." For some people, this is the only way they know how to say they care about someone. Their intent may be positive, but the effect is negative because there's a bite to their words.
- Then there are cases like Billy's: teasing or participating in someone else's teasing. Everyone is laughing except one person—the one being teased. If that person gets angry, he's accused of "not being able to take a joke."

A thought came to me one day when I was pondering this issue: Could I imagine Jesus ever discounting others? It would have been totally out of character for him, so I decided I wanted it to become out of character for me.

That decision occurred long before I gave up another behavior: discounting myself. Negative things I would never say to others seemed fine to say to myself, statements like, "How could you be so *stupid*?" Is there some reason to not do this, to not berate ourselves? Yes. Because even if we aren't hurting anyone else, we're hurting ourselves. And not only are other people children of God, but so are we. You and I.

The effects of discounting:

- Discounting wounds those who are discounted. Most of us have been debilitated to some degree by criticism and negative humor. They have damaged the person God created us to be. For instance, in our family, my very intelligent, albeit academically disinterested, youngest sister kept being compared with older, high-achieving siblings: "Why aren't you like your sisters?" was a refrain she heard so often from teachers it became a mantra. It took years of career success and eventual affirmation for her to quit believing she was dumb.
- Discounting diminishes trust. When I'm with someone who discounts me, I'm always on guard and rarely share my inner self. I'm braced for an axe to fall, for a put-down or a correction "for my own good." That kind of negative environment brings out the worst in me rather than the best. I avoid being with criticizers not so much because of who they are but, rather, because of who I am when I am with them.
- Discounting leads to anger and sometimes rage. In the Gospels, Jesus says, "If anyone strikes you on the

cheek, offer the other also" (Luke 6:29a). That is not a typical response. Instead, physical assaults often lead to anger and a desire to retaliate. The same holds true for blows to the heart and mind, which can wound even more than a slap in the face. They can anger us and give rise to an urge to strike back. Self-restraint may enable us to refrain from doing so at the moment, but eventually anger leaks out, most often directed at anyone who stumbles into the force field of our pain.

Discounting can be enmeshed in any relationship. I wince whenever I hear someone discount his or her spouse, or parents put down their child, or friends tease friends. Practice and a conscious effort can help us give up this behavior and, instead, affirm others. Following are four ways we can do that.

Ways We Affirm Others

1. *We affirm others when we listen to them.*
For me, being listened to by a spiritual companion is one of the great blessings of the relationship. No hidden agendas, no multitasking, no hurrying, just listening to whatever is on my heart and mind at the moment, anything that's important to me. What an affirmation—to simply be myself and have that be acceptable.

When we listen to others, we give them a gift: our undivided attention. This can help people get in touch with what their thoughts and feelings actually are. I've had a number of "ah-ha" experiences like that. I'll be talking about something and in the process of hearing myself speak, a light will go on in my head and I'll think, *I didn't know I felt this way.*

2. *We affirm others with our body language.*
My husband and I travel a lot and come in contact with many servers on land and sea. These hard workers used to be

invisible to me. Cabs were driverless. Rooms cleaned themselves. Prepared food appeared. Then one day while packing for a trip, I sensed God telling me to notice these people. Look at them. Smile. Acknowledge their existence. So I did.

Responses have been enlightening. For instance, when I smile at a hotel maid and say, "Hello," she usually looks startled, as if the thought that she's visible surprises her. Then comes a look of amazement that someone who recognizes her existence would care enough to smile. And finally comes a return smile, often a wide grin.

These are thirty-second encounters with strangers. With people we know, we have many opportunities to show them they are worthwhile. Lunching together; taking walks: gifts of time tell people we love them. And while we're together, focusing on them with an open mind and heart wordlessly says we value and honor what they're sharing.[1]

3. *We affirm others through honest feedback.*

I had a gift of writing long before I realized it. I wrote personal letters that people said touched them, and I figured that's what they said about any letter. I wrote letters to editors that got published and I thought that's what usually happened. Then one day I submitted an op-ed piece to a newspaper and they paid for it. Wow. Maybe I was…a writer. So I entered a literary contest. Much to my amazement, the entry won second place plus a cash award. This final affirmation—money—made something click in my brain: *I'm a writer*. The realization changed my life because it showed me where God was calling me.

My experience demonstrates a way to move into affirming someone: start with a compliment about something a person has done, then move into the gift beneath the compliment. A compliment tends to focus on objects ("Delicious pie.") or actions (Great touchdown!"). An affirmation often begins with the word *you* because it focuses on the person and his or her gifts ("You are a good cook."). People had been complimenting me for years about my writing. Some added that I was a good writer. Hearing this gave me a warm glow, but I didn't get the message that I had a gift and God was calling me to develop it. He wanted my writing to touch people's lives. Finally, perhaps in desperation, God sent money.

When giving feedback, the more specific it is the better, because vague affirmations ("Good job!") may look and feel hollow or meaningless. If what we're saying is significant, we want people to believe us and see themselves in a new light. In my experience, this rarely occurs instantly. As with my journey into a writing career, it often takes a number of affirmations for people to recognize and accept their giftedness.

4. *We can affirm others through prayer.*

Prayer is what differentiates spiritual companionship from other relationships, such as close friendships. Typically companions spend some time during a session praying for each other's needs. Within that prayer time, a prayer of affirmation expresses, out loud, gratitude for something one companion sees in the other.

So much can be said about prayer that I devote a chapter to it: chapter 10, "Praying with/for a Spiritual Companion." Here, I'll simply note several reasons the experience of affirmation through prayer can be transforming:

- It often is more easily received than affirmation given at other times. Walls are down, hearts are open to receiving.
- It strengthens people's self-esteem.
- It helps people see themselves as God sees them.
- It can lead to an awareness of God's presence right here, right now.

OBSTACLES TO AFFIRMATION

Affirmation is doable, free, and life-changing. So why isn't it widespread? Here are several reasons.

1. *We've never experienced it.*

In my mid-twenties, my friend Libby and I zipped through Europe in a new, red VW Beetle named Schnapsy. In Portugal, we became aware of several automotive hiccups. No problem; just find a mechanic. Found the mechanic. Then came the problem: He didn't speak English. We didn't speak Portuguese. Fortunately, Libby was a master at body language. Pointing to an engine part with oil on it, she scowled, frowned, shook her head, then moved on to the next item. Throughout her pantomime, the mechanic showed his understanding by nodding like a bobblehead doll. Within an hour, Schnapsy was as good as her three-week-old self again and we sped away.[2]

If you've never experienced affirmation, it's as much of a foreign language as Portuguese was for Libby and me. We couldn't speak it because we had never learned it, and we never learned it because we had never heard it.

The dilemma reminds me of what the late Archbishop Thomas Murphy once told a gathering of Catholic teachers. Urging them to develop their personal spiritual life, he said, "You can't give what you ain't got!" He was right, of course. When it comes to affirmation, we can't give any if we've never heard any. One way to hear them is through scripture.

The first chapter in the Bible tells us, "God saw everything that he had made, and indeed, it was very good" (Gen 1:31). Do we actually believe this? Can we accept our own goodness and that of others? Do we believe that God is pleased with us and that we are precious to him? Our ancestors had a hard time accepting this message from the prophets, so God sent Jesus to tell them and us. God asks us to pass on that news to others: We are loved. They are loved.

2. *Competitiveness, envy, jealousy*

In the movie *Amadeus*, Salieri, a hardworking, successful musician meets Mozart, a wild-haired young man with the laugh of a hyena. Is Salieri moved with joy when he first hears Mozart's music? He is not. Instead, he's shocked at how easily notes come to him, whereas Salieri has to slave away to achieve far less. It's not fair. He's devoted his life and music to God. Now here comes an irreverent, brilliant musician who upstages him. Salieri is jealous; he's envious; he broods. Consumed by these emotions, he decides to poison Mozart.

Nothing in history says Salieri killed Mozart, but the story touches on the age-old problem of how people respond to other people's gifts. It's as if God has a tiny storehouse of blessings to bestow on humankind. Giving you a gift means I get less. Naturally, I'll feel no desire to rejoice at what you have. Words of affirmation will not arise on my lips. Instead, I'll feel inferior to you.

James's epistle says, "Every good gift and every perfect present comes from heaven; it comes down from God" (Jas 1:17, GNT). Our infinite Creator has an infinite supply of blessings. Affirmation helps us discover them, develop them, then use them to build up one another and heal a broken world.

3. *Fear of pride*

In Mark Twain's novel *Tom Sawyer*, Tom tricks his friends into doing a task his Aunt Polly assigned to him: whitewashing a fence. When he shows her the finished product, she says, "Well I never! There's no getting around it, you *can* work when you're a mind to, Tom." And then she dilutes the compliment by adding, "But it's powerful seldom you're a mind to, I'm bound to say."[3]

If Aunt Polly had known how that fence actually got whitewashed, she might have praised Tom's ingenuity, then criticized his laziness, lest he become bigheaded. This can be a concern about affirmation—fear that the person we're affirming will become proud. Or fear that we ourselves will become self-centered if we accept an affirmation. In my experience, however, most people do not think too highly of themselves. Instead, most of us are quick to discount ourselves. We are blind to our dignity as children of God.

4. *An inability to receive affirmation from others*

Garrison Keillor's radio program, "Prairie Home Companion," always included a story about the mythical Minnesota town of Lake Wobegon. He sometimes spoke of their food and a cook's usual response to exclamations of joy about something sumptuous. No matter how much praise people lavished on her, the response invariably went something like this: "Oh, I don't know. There's just something 'off' about the flavor this time. It's a disappointment." In short, instead of receiving people's affirmations, cooks deflected them.

Jesus tells us, "It is out of the abundance of the heart that the mouth speaks" (Luke 6:45b). If affirmations from others bounce off us, we'll be empty of affirmations to offer anyone else. It reminds me again of Archbishop Murphy's words: "You can't give what you ain't got."

5. *Habit*

Thanksgiving dinner takes place each year at Aunt Maud's house at 4:00 p.m. sharp. Christmas trees must come down on December 31. Cousin Bob drinks too much at reunions. His two sisters don't speak to each other. They haven't done so since a silly argument years ago.

Relationship dynamics can become as much of a habit as turkey and pumpkin pie at Thanksgiving. Once established—like the sisters who haven't spoken in years—they're hard to change. This is how you *always* relate to this particular person. If teasing is the usual dynamic, switching to affirmation may feel awkward, if not impossible. Or perhaps your words will come across as phony, or people will think you're being phony, even though you're sincere. Result: words may feel stuck like a fish bone in your throat.

Or maybe no affirmations come to mind. You say to yourself, *I'm going to affirm my neighbor this week*. Wonderful idea. But no matter how hard you think, nothing comes to mind. Why? Probably because you're not used to seeing him in a new way, seeing him as God does. That's why, in my experience, affirmation comes more easily in new relationships than in long-established ones: their dynamics haven't become a habit.

AFFIRMATION: A WAY OF LIFE

For affirmation to become a way of life, we need to develop an attitude of reverence for ourselves and for others. Jesus is a model of what that means: He saw things in people they were unable to see for themselves. When he affirmed what he saw, they began to recognize their goodness, giftedness, and potential.

Take, for example, the Gospel of Luke's story of Zacchaeus. As Jericho's chief tax collector, he is a wealthy, despised man. Jesus is on his way through the town when he notices a short man looking down on him from a tree: Zacchaeus. Something about him must have touched Jesus because he stops, tells him to come down from the tree, and invites himself to be Zacchaeus's houseguest. What? This holy man wants to stay with a notorious sinner? Yes. By the time Jesus's visit is done, Zacchaeus is a new man who says, "Look, half of my possessions, Lord, I will give to the poor; and if I have defrauded anyone of anything, I will pay back four times as much" (Luke 19:8).

That's the power of affirmation, but it isn't self-generated. It's a gift from God that needs to be modeled and taught from generation to generation. Pray for this to become part of your spirituality and each of your relationships, including those you have with spiritual companions. Pray for the grace to be a person who models affirmation to others. A few guidelines:

- Avoid critical remarks. Many have a self-worth that is so wounded they are incapable of receiving negative criticism, even when it is legitimate and not a put-down. Many people are touchy because they have been psychologically beaten up in the past. Even a legitimate criticism causes them to flinch and shut down.
- Pray for yourself. Pray for the Holy Spirit to enable you to see yourself as God does and to become the person God desires you to be. Once you recognize that, affirmations to others will become possible.
- Offer affirmations. This takes a commitment to make God's love real to others and to yourself. It also requires a conscious effort. Don't be surprised if it's difficult at first. With time, it may come more readily and eventually become a way of life.

CONCLUSION

I would not be a writer and speaker today if it weren't for the affirmations of many patient, loving people. They saw beyond my initial awkwardness, errors, and stumbling efforts. As with those long-ago Wranglers at the University of Wisconsin, they emphasized pluses. They affirmed gifts I didn't know I had. They gave me eyes to see who I was and what God had given me. They changed my life.

That is affirmation's great gift. It changes other people's lives as well as your own. Becoming an affirming person can

- restore and strengthen your self-image;
- deepen your relationship with God because you will be more open to receiving God's tender love;
- effect your companion in healing, life-giving ways;
- spill out into your everyday life—to your family, to colleagues at work, to anyone you relate to in your life; and
- empower you to become more Christ-like, more like Jesus.

FOR YOUR REFLECTION

1. This chapter gives a three-step process for affirming others: (1) we see someone as God sees that person; (2) we allow ourselves to be moved by the goodness we see; (3) we show the person his or her goodness/giftedness. The appendix contains a list of affirmations—a few of the God-given gifts you may see in others. With or without using that list:

   a. Think of someone you know who's easy to be with, easy to like—a spouse, a child, a friend. Pray for the gift of affirmation, especially the ability to see this person as God does. Then say something to him or her or write an affirming note.

   b. Imagine going through the same process with someone who grates on your nerves, who *isn't* easy to be with. Pray to see this person as God sees him or her. Consider writing an affirming note, then decide whether or not to mail it.

2. How much experience have you had with discounting, either as a giver or a receiver of it?

   a. It's the rare individual who never discounts anyone. Assuming you are not that rare person, what is your tendency when you discount another person or yourself? (sarcasm, backhanded compliments, demeaning jokes, nicknames, etc.). If you would like to cut back on that behavior, ask God for the grace to do so; ask that discounting will become out of character for you. Initially, you may only recognize what you're doing. Later on, discounting simply won't fit who you are.

   b. When you've been a recipient of discounting, how have you responded—withdrawn; believed what was said; felt angry; avoided the one discounting you? Those are some typical responses. Imagine Jesus with you in one of those past situations. What is *his* response? What does he say to you? What do you say to him?

3. Think of a time someone affirmed you for one of your strengths/gifts. What impact has that affirmation had on you, your career, your relationships with others, your spiritual life?

4 Nearly all of Saint Paul's epistles begin with affirmation of the people receiving the letters. What follows are three examples. I invite you to reflect on one or more of them by imagining that Paul is writing directly to you:

   • Ephesians 1:16: "I do not cease to give thanks for you as I remember you in my prayers."

   • Philippians 1:3–4: "I thank my God every time I remember you, constantly praying with joy in every one of my prayers...."

- 2 Thessalonians 1:4: "We ourselves boast of you among the churches of God for your steadfastness and faith...."

Can you allow yourself to believe that Paul is addressing you? If this is difficult, spend a few minutes asking God for the grace to receive affirmations from others, including from Paul.[4]

Closing prayer

God of tenderness, thank you for seeing goodness in me. I ask for the grace to see goodness in others and reveal it to them. Amen.

CHAPTER 7

Endings

"FOR EVERYTHING THERE IS A SEASON"

IN THIS CHAPTER:

Introduction

Closure: "A time for every matter under heaven"

Eight reasons a companion relationship might end

Mini-endings

Moving forward

> For everything there is a season, and a time for
> every matter under heaven.
>
> —Ecclesiastes 3:1

Eva and I were spiritual companions for years. Even after she
moved to California, we often spoke by phone and sometimes

attended retreats together. One Friday I phoned to ask for her thoughts about grief. Her husband had died years earlier, and I was seeking wisdom for a presentation I was writing. What had helped her in the aftermath of his death? What had been unhelpful?

After talking for a few minutes, Eva said she had weekend house guests at the moment. Could she call me back on, say, Tuesday? "Of course," I said. "Talk to you then."

But I didn't talk to her then. On Sunday, Eva was killed in a car accident.

Relationships end for a variety of reasons, and the relationship of spiritual companions is no different. Some, like Eva's and mine, end abruptly. Others end with planning and prayer. Many end because of changing circumstances. Others simply fizzle out. A few cease because of conflict.

This chapter explores endings: the good, the bad, the feelings, the how-tos. It looks at closure. It also covers the importance of what, ideally, comes at the close of each companion session: a mini-ending. The goal here is maximum blessings, minimum pain, and an avoidance of mistakes.

CLOSURE: "A TIME FOR EVERY MATTER UNDER HEAVEN"

Closure is an ending that completes something. An ending that lacks closure is like a symphony without the final chord, a mystery novel without the last chapter. Something is missing.

Eva's death lacked closure. It shocked me to the core, all the more because the two of us hadn't been able to say a final goodbye. Thank God her family had a funeral for her. It helped us, the living, accept the ending. While the ritual and prayers gave me a chance for some closure, it naturally was one-sided. Eva was there in spirit, but her cremated remains were in a plain black container about the size and shape of a half-gallon carton of ice cream. So sad.

In the spiritual companion relationship, closure that's done well gives each person an opportunity to acknowledge that there was a time for this relationship and that time is over. Feelings naturally arise, many of them positive, especially gratitude for one another: the growth that has occurred because of this friendship; the laughter and the tears; the shared experiences of God; the mutual support. What gifts. What lasting memories.

Positive feelings like these can be expressed and celebrated during closure, along with negative ones such as grief, anxiety, and anger. Eva's death left a hole in my life. Who would replace the companionship we'd had for decades—the prayers, the deep conversations, the walks we took on retreats? I asked the question even though I knew the answer: every relationship is unique, so nobody could replace my friend. This awareness gave rise to anger at God. Couldn't he have prevented that senseless accident? Was that too much to ask? Eva was *too young* to die.

How can we do closure well so that each person moves forward in freedom, unimpeded by regrets or hurt feelings? I suggest a process:

1. Start by mutually agreeing that this is closure. Without that, the process may end without an ending—no final note.
2. Talk about feelings you each have, positive as well as painful. Avoid blame, tempting as that may be if companionship is ending for negative reasons. Just own your own feelings.
3. Close with prayer, asking God's blessings on each of you as you part.

This is the kind of process I went through with my coauthor, Father Leo Thomas, after we had worked together for eight years. We had a spiritual bond that had grown as we met weekly and wrote together. Now he was dying of cancer, and his life's work was complete.

To begin our last session, Leo and I both acknowledged that this was the end. We started with prayer, then Leo read a scripture passage, then we talked about our feelings and all that we had accomplished over the course of eight years. I started crying as I tried to read a prayer I had written, so Leo finished reading it for me. We ended by listening to an ancient prayer put to music.

Our ritual took about thirty minutes. The ending empowered me to move toward a beginning that included writing a third book, this time as a soloist. A final closure occurred several months later as I gave the eulogy at Leo's funeral.[1]

EIGHT REASONS A COMPANION RELATIONSHIP MIGHT END

Death certainly causes an unavoidable end to a companion relationship. More often it ends for other reasons. What follows are eight possibilities:

1. *Breaches of confidentiality.* As noted in chapter 4, spiritual companionship stands on a foundation of trust. Nothing destroys trust faster than the betrayal of a confidence. Even a single instance can wound a relationship deeply.
2. *Poor listening skills.* What if you listen deeply to your companion but he keeps checking his smartphone when you're sharing with him? Or what if his normal response is to give advice? Can this relationship last?

Only if a change occurs. (See chapter 5 for details about listening.)

3. *Spiritual imbalance or immaturity.* Spiritual companionship is meant to be a relationship of equals. What if you try to share your years of spiritual growth with someone who barely knows God? You're likely to end up feeling shortchanged and your friend may feel overwhelmed. Or you may inadvertently become a de facto spiritual director to her. Either way, your own needs won't be met.

4. *Lack of personal prayer.* If spiritual companionship is a friendship that includes Jesus as a third, important friend, he needs to be an important part of your individual lives. Chapter 8 covers personal prayer in detail. Here I will simply say that without an ongoing relationship with God that includes prayer, neither you nor your companion will be able to bring much to your sessions.

5. *Religious differences.* Being of different Christian denominations does not necessarily cause stress in a companion relationship. What will cause stress is a lack of respect for each other's faith traditions and practices. Any criticism of the other person's religion is out of line. So is an insistence on a tradition that's unique to one person's religion, such as a Catholic trying to persuade a companion to pray the Rosary during a session. Differences fade in importance when time together focuses on our commonality as Christians. The Holy Spirit unites us! We are brothers and sisters in the Lord.

6. *Neediness.* One of the blessings of spiritual companionship is the opportunity it gives us to bring our needs to God and experience him meeting us in those needs. Some people, however, are so wounded that it blocks their ability to focus on anything or anyone else.

Say, for example, your companion talks about her alcoholic husband at every session. He's unemployed; he's abusing her; the kids are fearful. She wants you to tell her what to do. No matter what you say or how you pray, nothing changes and your own needs aren't being met. That's because this person currently is too wounded to be a life-giving companion. She doesn't need you. She needs professional help and a support group.

7. *Low priority*. Chapter 2 looks at two features in any journey with God, one of which is showing up. The same holds true for a companion relationship. Both of you show up. You schedule get-togethers often enough to maintain your spiritual closeness. If sessions consistently fall into last place on either of your schedules, reexamine their value. Perhaps other responsibilities are making it impossible to be companions at this point. Perhaps it's time for an ending or just a temporary break.

8. *Drifting apart*. This often occurs when someone moves to another locale. The move doesn't necessarily mean the end of the relationship, but it does require more effort to keep it going—email updates, phone conversations, face-to-face contact via the Internet, perhaps get-togethers at retreats. Without any of those, the relationship might eventually devolve into mutual exchanges of Christmas cards.

MINI-ENDINGS (AKA, DEBRIEFING)

Basically, debriefing is a mini-ending for something that has just occurred, a way to ponder what has taken place.

When Leo and I began writing together, our sessions always started with twenty minutes of prayer; endings simply...ended.

After a couple of months, it became obvious that tensions were building. Leo was an introvert, I an extrovert; he was more thinking oriented, I was more toward the feeling end of the spectrum. These differences created possibilities for great work or great stress. Stress was winning out until we developed a debriefing process to end each session. We used it for eight years of work that gradually turned into a sentence-by-sentence collaboration on everything we wrote. Debriefing our sessions helped us learn how to work together as coauthors without stepping on each other's creativity. Two voices merged into one.

Debriefing is useful for the close of classes, retreats, and, yes, companion get-togethers. Here are several benefits:

1. Small problems can be resolved before they morph into big issues.
2. The good that has occurred can be recognized, affirmed, savored, and more easily remembered. This includes experiences of God that may have taken place.
3. From this arises the third benefit: spiritual growth.

Whenever my spiritual companion Meg and I meet, we end our session by asking two overall questions:

1. *Was anything unhelpful?* This question can cause squirmy feelings if something was, in fact, unhelpful. Temptation follows, the temptation to remain silent rather than gently bring up an issue such as nonlistening. What may feel safer—saying nothing—will eventually become a wall between two once-close companions. Or it may create a tension that ultimately erupts, Mt. Vesuvius-style. Loving honesty can prevent these problems by inviting discussion and increased awareness.
2. *What was the best thing about today's session?* Meg and I recognize the value of this question. However, whenever

I ask it at the end of teaching a class, I usually get blank looks. No matter. I persist because the question calls for a look inward to see what *was* the best thing that has just occurred. It's a way to remember the good for more than a moment, for it to be more than just a brief experience. It's a way to grow in wisdom and knowledge of the Lord and of so much else.

MOVING FORWARD

I used to walk in a wooded area in the foothills of the Cascade Mountains. There I always saw a brilliant pink flower beside the trail. Winter, spring, summer, or fall, it never faded, never died. Other plants blossomed, died, and bloomed again, but not that pink flower. It was plastic. It also was lifeless.

Real life constantly evolves, grows, withers, is reborn. Much as we might long to freeze-frame precious moments and close relationships to make them last forever, we can't. Instead, God calls us to accept reality—including our endings—and keep moving forward. One tool for doing that is to reflect on our experiences. It can give us the wisdom and courage to maintain what is maintainable and bid farewell to what isn't. Below are some possibilities.

FOR YOUR REFLECTION

1. What have been some of the endings in your life?
   a. Close relatives, friends, dating partners
   b. Careers, jobs

    c. People in your faith community (pastors, staff, community members, spiritual companions)
    d. Neighbors
    e. Others

2. Looking at the above:
    a. What were the most positive endings?
    b. What were the most painful?
    c. What have you learned from this chapter that could enable future endings to be less painful and more life-giving?

3. In closing, here is the ancient Celtic prayer that Leo and I prayed at the end of our eight years of working together. I invite you to use it for your own endings—and beginnings!—and for your relationship with God.

God Be in My Head

God be in my head and in mine understanding. God be in mine eyes and in my looking. God be in my mouth and in my speaking. God be in mine heart and in my thinking. God be at mine end and in my departing. Amen.

86

PART III
The Power
of Prayer

CHAPTER 8

Personal Prayer

Pray in the Spirit at all times in every prayer and supplication.

—Ephesians 6:18

INTRODUCTION:
THE MYSTERY OF GOD

My father's cousin Elizabeth Rooney inherited a Wisconsin farm that included Cave of the Mounds on its property. As children, my brothers and sisters and I toured it each time we visited the farm. Years passed. We grew up. One year during a family reunion in Madison, all of us decided to revisit the cave. Elizabeth's husband, Mike, gave us a private tour.

Midway through the tour, Mike suggested that he turn off all the lights so we could experience total darkness—something that's only possible in a cave. A bit hesitantly, we agreed.

I'll never forget the experience of being plunged into a complete absence of light. I knew my family was present, but I couldn't see them. Blindness made me feel disoriented, almost dizzy from the loss of one of my senses. Instinctively the six of us drew together in a nervous huddle, then gave a collective sigh of relief when the lights came on again. Whew! Eyesight, walls, a path leading to a known destination.

God is always totally present to us, more present than my family was in that cave. But I can't *see* him any more than I could see them. That complicates things because it immerses me in a mystery beyond my senses and control. Nevertheless, I am committed to the Lord. This chapter explores an essential aspect of our relationship with God: personal prayer.

DIFFERENT WAYS TO FOCUS

Sunday school taught me that the One I worship is a tri-une God: three persons in one God—Father, Son, and Holy Spirit. An analogy offered to describe this was a triangle. I also learned that God loves us and invites each of us to enter into a relationship with him. I struggled with this because how could I love a triangle, for heaven's sake?

Eventually, I realized that my brain could focus on only one person of the Trinity at a time. In different circumstances, I needed, and was open to, a different aspect of God.

God the Father

Here is the Creator of the stars and planets, the mountains and oceans, the trees and flowers. This is the One whose first words brought light into the darkness of nothingness, who said, "'Let there be light'; and there was light" (Gen 1:3). What an unfathomable power.

I tend to experience the Creator when I'm outdoors and see a beauty that takes away my breath, perhaps a rose in full bloom or a sunset blazing with color across the sky. At times like this, a prayer of thanksgiving arises within me as I see beyond creation to its Creator. Some call this "nature prayer."

In times of great darkness, I turn to this all-powerful Person of the Trinity. I need assurance that Someone far greater than I can handle what is happening. The morning after 9/11 was one such occasion. Feeling shattered, traumatized, and grieved, at dawn I walked to the top of a hill and looked out onto the Cascade Mountains and Lake Washington. "Lord," I prayed, "if you are big enough to create these mountains and these stars and this sky and this lake, I believe you are greater than the horrible thing that has happened to America. Help us, Lord. We need you."

God the Son

Here is Jesus, the One who came to dwell among us two thousand years ago, who knows what it feels like to be hungry, thirsty, tired, and sweaty. Here is the Savior who says, "I am the light of the world. Whoever follows me will never walk in darkness but will have the light of life" (John 8:12).

The risen Lord tends to be my focus during daily prayer. He's my warm, safe Jesus, the One who has promised to be with me always, no matter what (Matt 28:20). He consoles me when I'm sad, calms me when I'm anxious, encourages me when I'm reluctant, strengthens me when I'm weak and, yes, shines a light of truth on me when I get off base.

God the Holy Spirit

Here is the One who came upon the disciples at Pentecost and empowered them to spread God's message everywhere. For me, the third person of the Trinity does feel like a power: the power to love, to reach out to suffering people, to discern the best course of action in given situations, and then do what I have discerned.

As a writer, I sometimes experience the Holy Spirit when I get into a creative space that fills me with joy. It took years for me to name this and recognize it as a shared joy with God. The Spirit and I are sharing the joy of cocreating something beautiful. What a gift and what a privilege.

WHEN TO PRAY

Chapter 2 looked at the importance of spiritual companions in a relationship with God. That's one ingredient. Another, equally important ingredient is private time with the Lord. When do we do this? Here's one scenario:

You are having a dreadful day. Your boss just fired you; your car is making bad, expensive-sounding noises; you feel like you're coming down with the flu; you're alone and—I don't know how this happens—but somehow you find yourself hanging from a cliff by your fingers. Wouldn't this be a good time for a little prayer?

In the above scene, I would suggest one word: "Help!" For the first several decades of my life, that about summed up my prayer life: I turned to God when I needed something. I still do this and that's fine. But God longs for more. God longs for a *relationship* with each of us. The One who is Love longs for our love.

Spiritual companions support and enhance each other's journey with God. For me, this is the relationship's main benefit. During sessions with my companion, Meg, the two of us do our best to open our hearts and minds to God, including during prayer. But we meet monthly and both recognize that's not enough time with the Lord. We know that for our sessions to bear fruit, each of us needs to create space in our lives for personal prayer, ideally every day.

HOW TO PRAY

Now comes that age-old question: How do we pray? "Lord, teach us to pray," said Jesus's disciples (Luke 11:1). So he taught them the Lord's Prayer—one I often pray. But other options exist too. My book *Healing: Stories of Faith, Hope, and Love* includes individual chapters on seven types of prayer and how to say them. What follows is a brief description of each:[1]

1. *Prayer of petition/intercession.* That prayer you offer while hanging from a cliff by your fingers—that's a *prayer of petition*: asking God for something you need. (If a friend was the one hanging from the cliff, it would be a *prayer of intercession*: asking on behalf of your friend.)

   With this ever-popular type of prayer, we lift up a need to the Lord and seek his help. Requests may be minor: "Help me with this test." They may be major:

"Heal my uncle's cancer." They may be about personal needs: "Show me where to find a job," or global ones: "Lord, save the people in Syria." Large or small, personal or global, the goal with any concern isn't to persuade a stingy deity to do what we want. Instead, we do our best to release a need into God's care, trusting in his help to bring about the most loving result possible in that situation.

2. *Contrition*. This is not a very popular prayer—"I'm sorry. Forgive me. I have sinned." Finding a sin within ourselves can make us feel…bad. We're hardwired to avoid pain, yet Jesus urges us to "repent, and believe in the good news" (Mark 1:15). Why do that? Because contrition liberates us. Confronting our sins frees us to do the opposite: choose life.

Through repentance, God gives us the grace to change the direction in which we've been seeking happiness. Sin has led us away from God. Contrition turns us toward the Author of joy, the One who always wants what is best for us, even when it may not feel that way.

3. *Scripture meditation*: This can open the heart and mind to experiencing God speaking personally to each of us. A number of ways exist for doing this.

I sometimes select a passage in my Bible and imagine God is addressing me. If a name is given, I substitute my own, for example, "Have no fear, my servant Jacob….For I am with you, says the LORD, to save you" (Jer 30:10a, 11). Inserting my own name instead of Jacob's helps me experience God's presence. This calms my spirit and enables me to deal with whatever is distressing me.

4. *Centering/contemplative prayer*. This is prayer beyond words, images, or thoughts—easy to define, hard to do. "Be still, and know that I am God!" says the

Psalmist (Ps 46:10a), but the ever-active brain resists. Questions about a problem; feelings about a family member; thoughts about a recent TV drama: these are distractions. Some are as annoying as a barking dog. Others may be an enjoyable daydream, perhaps one where you're a fearless fighter whose heroism averts a disaster. Applause! Accolades! Ah, but you turn aside praise because you are, after all, humble.

Welcome or not, distractions take us away from this prayer's goal: union with God. To quiet the mind, contemplatives recommend choosing a sacred word (called a "mantra" by some)—perhaps a name for God, a phrase from scripture, or a word such as *love*. Quietly repeating the sacred word helps us refocus on God's presence within us when thoughts or images intrude.

5. *Prayer of praise.* Praise is a natural response to a positive event such as a football victory or a stirring concert. The prayer of praise focuses on God, acknowledging God's great kindness and goodness to us. The Book of Psalms overflows with praise, including in its final verse: "Let everything that breathes praise the LORD! Praise the LORD!" (150:6).

Praise comes easily to me during a positive event. It's far more difficult during a crisis. Yet this is when I most need to trust that God is in charge and sees beyond my limited vision. It's when I need to believe the words of Saint Paul: "We know that all things work together for good for those who love God" (Rom 8:28).

6. *Spiritual journaling.* Cardinal John Henry Newman called this type of prayer "praying through the tip of a pen." It's a way to express our inner being and also to free ourselves from thoughts going around endlessly on the racetrack of the mind. We may discover parts

of ourselves we didn't know existed. That, in turn, can lead to a deeper connection with God.

Spiritual journaling can be a poem, a song, a drawing, a letter to God, a response to a scripture passage—in short, any form of self-expression.

7. *Music, art, and movement.* These prayers have the power to do an end-run around our intellect and reach into the depths of our being. We use our God-given senses to worship the Creator of those senses.

- *Hearing*: Whose spirit has never soared at the sound of a favorite song? We may hear the music in a concert hall; or it may come from our own voice as we sing in the shower.

- *Sight*: Whose heart has never been touched by a child's drawing, or a flower in bloom, or a sculpture in a museum? Art can be God made (nature) or human made, including our own creative expressions.

- *Movement*: Dancing, standing, running, bowing, kneeling, walking. Using our body to pray can be an exhilarating experience, not unlike the runner in the movie *Chariots of Fire* who told his sister that when he ran swiftly, he felt God's joy.

I believe God is present in intense moments like these, whether it's sight or sound or movement. The Lord is with us in whatever we are experiencing, whether it's joyful or painful. Our challenge is to recognize this and respond.

OBSTACLES TO PERSONAL PRAYER

Personal prayer unites us with a Mystery beyond ourselves. And, in the words of Alfred Lord Tennyson, "More things are wrought by prayer than this world dreams of." If true, why isn't the whole world praying every day for needs both large and small? What follows are three common reasons: lack of time, boredom, and self-criticism.

1. *Lack of time*

It's morning and you're about to dive into an ultra-busy day—urgent needs, a doctor's appointment, and more. Now the phone rings as you're walking out the door. It's a man from your bank. "Good news!" he says. "Your great-uncle Charlie died and left you a million dollars. But there's a deadline: You need to come in and sign for the money today. Do you have time to do this?"

In my experience, prayer yields results worth much more than a million dollars. The problem is, results occur over the course of years, not days. They may or may not include careers or money. They usually enhance relationships beyond the one we develop with God. This can lead to inner strength and peace. But before that can happen, there's that pesky problem: lack of time.

If Gallup ever does a survey to find out who wants to be alone with God each day, I'll bet 90 percent of prayer wannabes will give the same answer as to why they don't: no time. And I'll bet they imagine that somewhere out there are folks with blank schedules who do have time to pray. Perhaps there are a few. For the rest of us, it's a time struggle.

Personal prayer is a lifestyle decision, similar to choices such as diet and exercise. They either become a habit or a daily wrestling match: To exercise or not; if yes, when? To pray or not; if yes, when? Choices like these exhaust me. It's like getting up in the morning wanting to clean the house. But first there's another task, then another, and another. Time and tasks march along until the sun sets, and I feel drained because of the energy I've put into cleaning the house. In fact,

SEEKING *Christ* THROUGH *Friendship*

dust balls and grime remain because all I've done is expend a lot of energy thinking about cleaning.

Some people handle this issue by deciding to pray all day, to develop an ongoing God consciousness and talk to him throughout the day. That's good. Jesus did this—for instance, praying before he raised Lazarus from the dead (John 11:1–44). But the Gospels show us that Jesus also spent time alone with his Father, his Abba:

> In the morning, while it was still very dark, he got up and went out to a deserted place, and there he prayed. And Simon and his companions hunted for him. When they found him, they said to him, "Everyone is searching for you." (Mark 1:35–37)

Poor Jesus: hounded by needy people. It reminds me of children's demands, or the expectations in some work environments. It's easy to surrender and let others determine how we live each moment. Or we can carve out a daily block of time for prayer so our internal resources don't dry up. We can make prayer a habit. If even the Son of God needed this in order to recharge his mental, emotional, and spiritual batteries, I figure I do too. As little as fifteen minutes renews me and helps me remain centered throughout the day.

2. *Boredom*

Mark 9:2–8 recounts a mountaintop experience that Peter, James, and John had with Jesus: the transfiguration. It featured white garments, an appearance by Elijah and Moses, a cloud overshadowing them, and a voice saying, "This is my Son, the Beloved; listen to him!" (verse 7b). Wouldn't it be great if every prayer time was so soul-stirring? Wouldn't it be great if it would last? Peter expressed that desire: "Rabbi, it is good for us to be here; let us make three dwellings, one for you, one for Moses, and one for Elijah" (verse 5). In short, why return to the grittiness of real life? Let's stay here.

Alas, in any relationship, experiences like these are rare, and a relationship with God is no different. It's like a life-giving marriage or friendship: many ordinary, even sometimes boring, moments, along with a few glorious ones. Day-to-day life may simply feel familiar and grounded, interspersed with occasional highs.

If prayer was a fabulous experience every time we sat down with the Lord, we'd probably find a way to fit it into our lives each day, no matter how busy our schedule. But then that might become the reason to pray—for the buzz, not the relationship. Instead, I believe God is pleased when we pray more for love of him than for love of mountaintop experiences.

So personal prayer times can bore us because they're too ordinary. But here's another possibility: we may be using styles of prayer that don't match our personality. We don't change who we are when we pray. For instance, introverts outside of prayer are also introverts within their prayer times. Their efforts are more likely to bear fruit when they use prayer styles that appeal primarily to introverts, such as contemplation.[2]

I've often heard contemplation called "the highest form of prayer." Not necessarily. I'm an extrovert with a sleep disorder so, for me, contemplative prayer times fluctuate between deep sleep and utter boredom. Worse yet, the sessions bear no fruit in my life beyond prayer. That's how to determine the highest form of prayer for each of us: not the one that feels best while we pray, but rather the one that shows results *outside* our prayer times: Greater awareness of God-moments. More patience. Better choices. More inner peace.

To figure out which prayer styles suit us best, there's no need to analyze our personality. We'll naturally gravitate toward those that match who we are. What is essential, however, is learning different styles of prayer and then doing them.

I never would have known that scripture meditation was my favorite form of prayer if I hadn't learned its basics and tried it for awhile.

3. *Self-criticism*

Saint Paul told the Romans, "We do not know how to pray as we ought" (Rom 8:26b). I nod my head and say, "Certainly." Yet if I get distracted when I pray, or if my prayers feel "blah," a part of me believes I haven't prayed well.

Self-criticism in any area of life is a hard habit to shake. Prayer is no exception. I liken it to being a skater in the Olympics where, on a great day, we soar into the lead. Everyone cheers; we smile and wave. On a bad day, the score plunges. Murmurs of sympathy come from the stands; TV stations endlessly replay our errors; we cry.

Of course when it comes to prayer, we're the ones doing the scoring and replays, not God. Recalling a verse from the Letter of James may help at times like this: "All that is good is given us from above; it comes down from the Father of all light" (Jas 1:17a, NJB). If the act of praying is good, then every prayer time, great or not so great, is a gift. It may feel as if we're giving God a gift when, in fact, God is gifting us.

Prayer takes you and me into the mystery of finite creatures relating with an infinite Creator. Tempting as it may be to focus on our skill, that's not important. Instead, what counts is the decision to pray. We show up, with or without feelings of enthusiasm. God always delights in our presence and welcomes us with the kind of joy the father of the prodigal son showered upon his long-lost returning child (Luke 15:11–32).

A major challenge in prayer is to set aside expectations, quit being self-critical, quit apologizing to God. If we continually browbeat ourselves for the quality of our prayer times, eventually one of two things will happen: we'll either quit praying because we say we're no good at it, or we'll avoid our deepest self.

In my experience, people who steer clear of their own depth often are afraid of what lies within. It may be self-hatred or anger at someone else, including God. It may be soul-searing pain. It may be denial of an addiction. Whatever the cause, the result locks wounded people into a shallow life both within and beyond prayer. Time alone with God may become a hollow performance while life outside of prayer feels meaningless. It, too, may become a performance.

"YOU WILL KNOW THE TRUTH…"

Tina and I were spiritual companions when she lived in Seattle. During our gatherings she sometimes talked about her mother, who never passed up an opportunity to tell her daughter what a disappointment she was, how she couldn't do anything right. She also demanded Tina's time: drive here, buy this, do that. It never ended. Then came advancing age and a risk of living alone.

One day, Tina arrived for our get-together looking cheerful in a nervous sort of way. She chatted about little things during lunch, then in a by-the-way fashion, mentioned she had invited her mother to live with her and her husband.

My jaw dropped. "Wait," I said. "You've told me your mother is mean. She orders you around. She's critical. Let's talk about this invitation."

Tina apparently had no desire to do that. Instead, she looked at her watch and said, "Oh, look the time. Gotta run." With that, she stood up, said goodbye, gathered her belongings, put on her coat, and dashed out the door. My jaw remained dropped. What was *that*? Lacking any knowledge about what "that" might be, I prayed for Tina by myself. I asked God to be with her and help her deal with her mother. This became part of my personal prayer times, support for my companion between sessions.

Jesus told his followers, "You will know the truth, and the truth will make you free" (John 8:32). Before we get too gleeful and giddy about this promise, it may help to know there's usually a gap between knowing a truth and being set free by it. When we're emotionally, spiritually, or relationally wounded, a journey of weeks, months, or even years is typical.

Such was the case with Tina. Her mother had emotionally abused her throughout her whole life. Tina had coped by being an obedient daughter, doing everything she thought would please Mom. Perhaps inviting Mom to live in their home would finally bring forth the love she longed for.

The countdown to move-in day began and, as Tina later told me, with it came a growing sense of dread. She felt trapped. Why had she done such a stupid thing? How could she get out of it? But it was too late, she thought. Invitations are irreversible. She was going to have to live an endless nightmare with this mean person forever, and it was her fault.

Dread became desperation. Tina's emotions spiraled downward until she found herself thinking that getting run over by a car and dying would solve her problem. When this began to sound like a good idea, she suddenly snapped out of it, picked up the phone, called her doctor, and asked for an emergency appointment.

Severe wounds and those that persist despite our best efforts often benefit from—and sometimes require—outside help. Tina's doctor told her in no uncertain terms that she needed to immediately disinvite her mother. His authority as a physician gave her permission to undo what she thought was undoable. Her mother protested the reversal and threw guilt at her daughter: "You have wounded me to the quick," she said.

With the doctor's words in mind, Tina remained firm. No living with them. Instead, she offered to help search for a retirement home. In the end, they located a lovely place where her mother spent the last few years of her life. One day she said, "I wish I had come here a long time ago."

Personal prayer is a key ingredient in our spiritual journey. During Tina's crisis, her prayers had been like those of a drowning person: "Help, help, help." Jesus was a lifeguard, but where was he anyway? Did he notice she needed to be saved? After her mother was happily living in her new home, deep prayer became possible again for Tina, like the blooming of a once-dormant tree. So glorious.

LOOKING AHEAD

Whether it's a crisis like Tina's or simply everyday life, spiritual companions offer each other vital support. They share their lives and pray together about what is on their hearts and minds. That is the subject of the next chapter.

FOR YOUR REFLECTION

In prayer, no matter how proficient we become or what type of prayer we use, we aren't seeking competence. We're seeking God. That's the goal in all the seasons of our life. The following may help:

1. When you pray, what is your focus? How do you often envision God?

SEEKING *Christ* THROUGH *Friendship*

2. Looking at the seven types of prayer described in this chapter, how many of them—or others—have you ever tried?
   a. Which are the most life-giving for you? Which are the least effective?
   b. What options do you have for learning types of prayer you've never tried? (*Healing: Stories of Faith, Hope, and Love* is one possibility.)
3. This chapter looks at three obstacles to personal prayer.
   a. How do you, or can you, carve out a few minutes per day for alone time with God? What works best for you?
   b. Do you ever find prayer so boring that you want to give up? When tempted to do so, ask God for the gift of perseverance and, perhaps, some clue that prayer is bearing fruit in your life.
   c. Do you ever criticize yourself for the quality of your prayer times? That's normal! When this occurs, pray for self-acceptance and, yes, humility.
4. Jesus's promise: "You will know the truth and the truth will make you free." Is that a scary idea for you? If so, pray for the courage to enter more fully into your deeper self.

In closing, here is a poem by Elizabeth Rooney, the Wisconsin cousin and owner of Cave of the Mounds described at the beginning of this chapter.

I spend so much time
Feeling around in the dark,
Hoping that I will blunder
Into the arms of God.

104

Personal Prayer

The times of silence
And the child-like self denials,
The attempts at half-understood
Varieties of prayer,
The falling down and getting up again—
All, all are intended
Somehow to help me
Fumble my way toward Him.

I believe in a Reality
Beyond my comprehension and my touch
And I want to be where He is.
I have never wanted anything as much.[3]

CHAPTER 9

Sharing with a Companion

IN THIS CHAPTER:

Sharing during a companion session

Basic question: Where is God in my life?

Possible topics for sharing

> Where two or three are gathered in my name, I am
> there among them.
>
> —Matthew 18:20

Henry Thoreau once wrote, "I have never found the companion
that was so companionable as solitude."[1] Well OK, this was a
man who spent twenty-six months alone in a cabin—a hermit.
But only for awhile. And even during his Walden Pond years,
Thoreau remained in close contact with family and friends.

Who knows the details of what they said or did when they got together.`` What matters is what we who are spiritual companions say and do when we meet. This chapter looks at one of our two primary activities: sharing together.

SHARING DURING A COMPANION SESSION

Spiritual companion sessions usually start with a time of mutual sharing. This leads into praying about what has been shared.[2] Normally one of my companions, Tina, and I followed that pattern. We'd have lunch together while talking about what was going on in our lives. However, as noted in the previous chapter, no prayer time occurred after Tina said she had invited her mother to live with her and her husband. When I suggested we talk a bit more about the invitation, she fled. No discussion, no prayer.

This brings up an important point: *Each companion decides what to share.* I suggested to Tina that we talk about a subject she had raised. Based on her response, it didn't take a PhD in psychology for me to realize this was too painful for her to deal with at the moment. A couple of months later, we did talk and pray about it, but not until after she had received professional help, disinvited her mother, and started searching for a retirement home for her.

BASIC QUESTION: WHERE IS GOD IN MY LIFE?

Look at people rushing around, multitasking, complaining (or boasting) about how busy they are. Then ask yourself if these people are noticing something important: their own life. Perhaps you and I occasionally suffer from the same absence of self-awareness. If so, we're unlikely to ask a more challenging question: Where is God in my life?

Companion sessions give us an opportunity to ponder our life and how God fits into it, then share our thoughts and experiences with a fellow sojourner. This helps us do what Presbyterian minister Frederick Buechner urges us to do: "Listen to your life. See it for the fathomless mystery it is...because in the last analysis all moments are key moments, and life itself is grace."[3]

Jesus tells us, "Remember, I am with you always, to the end of the age" (Matt 28:20b). In other words, he is with us each moment of the day and night, not just at church and not just when we're praying. The Savior of the world wants to be involved in *every* aspect of our life, to be included in everything we think, feel, say, and do.

- Does Jesus care if you impulsively invited a relative to live with you and now feel trapped? Yes.
- Does God care if your job has left you feeling burned out? Yes.
- Does he care about your struggles with anger about your neighbor? Yes. Does he have something to say to you about that issue? Probably.
- Does he care about your health problem—one that the medical community can't figure out or treat? Yes.
- Does Jesus grieve with you at the loss of a loved one? Yes, yes.

Our challenge is to recognize God's presence in our assorted situations, both small and big. This is one of the great blessings of spiritual companions. They open our eyes to what we otherwise might miss.

108

What, then, do we share during any given session? Usually we talk about what's happening in our life at the moment. Here are some ideas to reflect on before a get-together:

- What am I concerned about these days? What is on my mind or in my heart?
- Where is God in this? How am I experiencing God with me? Or perhaps, *am* I experiencing God in this?
- What does God want?

Given the range of topics we might think about on any given day, it's good to eliminate a few categories when considering what to share during a session. The following are some suggestions:

- Sports: "How 'bout those Seahawks?!"
- Political opinions: "Can you believe what Congress just did?
- Gossip: Inappropriate at any time. It does not make Jesus smile.

Topics like these keep us on the surface of life. They distract us by drawing our attention outward. They may momentarily energize us and give us a sense of involvement in life, but in the end, they consume time without helping us deepen our relationship with God or anyone else. They also will fail to empower us to move forward on our spiritual journey. So instead of the above distracting topics, what follows are ideas to consider.

POSSIBLE TOPICS FOR SHARING

1. *Your prayer life*

SEEKING *Christ* THROUGH *Friendship*

This could be about your faithfulness to prayer or your progress in it. Another option: prayer experiences that you've had. These may have occurred during a prayer time or at any time of the day or night, perhaps in a dream.

For instance, during the tumultuous 2016 election months I found myself feeling so stressed I could barely sleep. One morning I reflected on several verses from Psalm 62: "Rest in God alone, my soul! He is the source of my hope. He alone is my rock, my safety, my stronghold, so that I stand unwavering" (vv. 5–6, NJB).

As I pondered this passage, I realized I had become addicted to the news: incessantly checking the Internet, radio, and TV, feeling empty and anxious if I didn't. If I had had a smartphone, it would have been an additional body extremity. I craved being "in the know" like an alcoholic craves a drink. The endless drama of the campaign and the election had lured me into turning my energy outward rather than inward. I needed to find peace in God rather than in the news.

Before meeting with my companion, Meg, here's what I journaled about the above situation: "I'm never at peace. I'm always in turmoil. I believe my senses more than I believe in God. The above psalm gives a different message: 'God alone is my rock, my safety, my stronghold.' If I keep my eyes focused on God, rather than on the news, maybe my soul and mind will begin to believe it. Lord, I do believe. Help my unbelief!" (see Mark 9:24).

Sharing this journal entry with Meg helped later when the two of us sat down to pray. I had clearly stated my dilemma; Meg knew what was on my mind, how I felt, what I wanted to pray about. Therefore we were able to focus on that particular situation during the time we prayed for my needs.

2 *Important relationships*

Family, friends, neighbors, colleagues at work: These, and others, are fertile ground for topics to raise during a companion session. In Tina's case, her mother fit into this category. Just thinking about her had made Tina want to flee—which she literally had done after initially telling me about her invitation.

By the time we met again, Tina had met with her physician and issued a retraction to her mother. She would not be living with them. Now Tina was ready to talk—how she regretted the invitation as soon as the words left her mouth; how her husband liked the invitation because it would bring in rent money; about her growing panic and thought of escaping by getting run over by a car; about her doctor's insistence that she disinvite her mother; about her feelings of relief after doing so. Now, Tina said, she and her husband and mother were searching together for a retirement home for her mother.

Few topics in a companion session rise to the level of Tina's stress and panic. Typically, we have many relationships in our lives that we might talk about. How do we choose one? For me, it usually comes down to who is in my heart and on my mind at the moment. What's going on in our relationship? I might want to cover many people in a grand sweep of cocktail party depth but that doesn't work. One relationship at a time is usually the limit.

Now comes temptation: the temptation to talk only about that person. This can easily slip into problem-solving, gossip, complaining, or just news unless we keep our focus where it should be: on the people in the room—the spiritual companions. Tina spoke about her mother while I listened intently, but eventually the conversation came back to her as I asked a few questions such as what her feelings were, both then and now. What triggered the invitation in the first place? How had she prayed during the panic time? (Answer: "Mostly just, 'help, help, help, help'"—an excellent choice of prayer, one I always pray during, say, a Seattle earthquake.)

If Tina and I had talked only about her mother, we would have had little or nothing to pray about afterward in terms of her spiritual journey. That's why, when looking at a relation-ship, it's important to periodically ask this: Are we focusing our eyes and energy on the people in the room right now? Or on someone who isn't here? If it's the latter, discussion can turn into a complaint session, endlessly recycling what's hap-pening, blaming other people. Why is that a problem? Why not air grievances? Because *complaining has no power*. It gives the illusion of accomplishing something when, in reality, it dis-tracts us from our inner journey with God and draws us away from a power that we do have: the power of prayer.

    3. *Worries and fears*

A recent cartoon shows Garfield the cat strolling along. In the second frame, he walks past a sign that says, "Beware of pretty much everything." In the final frame, he thinks, *Like there needs to be a sign*.

Indeed. And if we lack ideas for what to beware of—what to fear and worry about—entire industries exist to help us find a few more perils. They can stop us in our tracks, make us feel trapped, consume our energy, tempt us to run from real or imagined danger. We can become like Elijah who fled to the desert and prayed for death when he heard that an enraged Queen Jezebel had put a price on his head. Asked by God why he was in hiding, Elijah gave a litany of reasons including the faithlessness of the Israelites. He ended with, "I alone am left, and they are seeking my life, to take it away" (1 Kgs 19:10). God assured the prophet that he wasn't alone. Seven thousand Israelites were still faithful. Strengthened by that knowledge, Elijah set out and selected one of those faithful ones, Elisha, who became his companion and successor.

Aloneness. For me, that's one of the most painful aspects of fear and worry. It heightens emotions and increases their power. Voicing our feelings to a compassionate listener can remove a lot of that isolation. This is a great gift that a spiritual companion can give us, the gift of simply listening with love.

4. *Use of God's gift of time*

A woman once told me about a Christian young man who had moved in with her and her family. Shortly after his arrival she saw him sunbathing on their porch. "What are you doing?" asked this mother of five young children. "Why aren't you working on a couple of chores that my husband has pointed out to you?"

"I'm waiting for the Lord to tell me what to do today," he replied.

How creative—a new variation on work avoidance. But a number of sincere followers of Christ do believe that God wants to tell them everything they should do every day. Household tasks, TV programs to watch, store purchases, sightseeing options: these all need God's stamp of approval.

I have two problems with this approach to deciding how to use God's gift of time. First, I believe it takes away free will and the ability to grow and use our intelligence in mature, loving ways. For instance, the young man in the above story already had a to-do list that spelled out the help this family needed. He could have used his free will to choose the task he felt most capable of doing, or the one that was least odious to him, or the one that looked the most urgent. Something. Anything. Instead, he failed to consider the possibility that God had already communicated to him through a list. What he needed to do now was pick a task and start working.

My second problem with seeking God's direction for every moment of a day: It removes responsibility for decisions. *I* didn't decide to buy this or do that. God told me to do it. This gives every choice an aura of divine approval, and how can anyone call *that* into question? The decision was God's, not mine.

Using time well for daily matters usually is instinctive and doesn't require further instructions. I exercise; I shop; I travel; I write; I choose what to watch on TV. God is with me in all these moments, wanting me to make life-giving choices while also giving me the freedom to learn, grow, make mistakes, fall down, get up, and learn some more. This is the spiritual journey.

Companions can help when time becomes a problem. Sharing an issue brings it into the light of day. Verbalizing it can lead to clarity and be an excellent lead-in to prayer. For instance:

- You feel like a slave to your smartphone. It occupies almost every waking hour.
- Your newly retired spouse is driving you crazy by following you around all day. You feel smothered. You need time for yourself.
- You can't seem to find time for daily prayer in your ultra-busy life.

God does care about our use of time, but I don't think he tells us what to do on an hour-by-hour basis. Which brings us back to the young man: How did the harried mother respond to his excuse? "While you're waiting to hear from God," she said, "the lawn needs mowing."

FOR YOUR REFLECTION

1. This chapter begins with a basic question: "Where is God in my life?" Where is God in *your* life right now? I suggest using this chapter to answer that question. For instance: What are you concerned about right now?
2. This chapter also covers four possible topics for sharing with a companion. Have you ever talked about

any of the following with someone close to you? If so, how did they respond?

a. Your prayer life.

b. Important relationships.

c. Worries and fears.

d. Your use of time. (Chapter 12—"Discernment"— covers this topic in greater detail.)

3. What God told the Israelites holds true for us as we decide how to use each day's gift of time: "I have set before you life and death, blessings and curses. Choose life so that you and your descendants may live" (Deut 30:19b).

a. Where are you choosing life on a regular, often daily, basis (for example, exercising, wholesome entertainment, high priority on relationships)?

b. Where are you struggling to choose life? Which ones do you feel like sharing with your spiritual companion (for example, poor diet, too much TV, neglect of relationships)?

4. In closing, a prayer:

Lord, thank you for your constant presence with me. I ask for the courage to share my spiritual life with a companion. Help me choose what to talk about. Enable me to safely share my thoughts and feelings with this person. Give my companion listening ears and a loving heart. Amen.

CHAPTER 10

Praying with/for a Spiritual Companion

IN THIS CHAPTER:

Why pray with and for a companion?

Two foundations for shared prayer

When to pray

What to pray for

"Lord, teach us to pray"

> Devote yourselves to prayer, keeping alert in it with thanksgiving. At the same time pray for us as well.
>
> —Colossians 4:2–3a

One Saturday afternoon, Meg and her husband Nels were with a group serving a hot meal to homeless men when Nels suddenly collapsed with a heart attack. Emergency! Call 911, bring in the medics, get Nels to the hospital, stabilize his heart, admit him to the hospital.

Now came another urgent task, this one for Meg: deal with medical insurance. She phoned me one morning to say she had to go to three places but felt the need for support. Could I go with her? I had a flexible schedule, so I was able to immediately say, "Sure. How about if I drive?"

First stop: Nels's former place of employment. Before going in, I suggested to Meg that we pray together. So we sat in the car for a few minutes, held hands, and asked for an outpouring of the Spirit on us and on everyone we would meet that day. We prayed out loud, we prayed silently, we prayed for a day of miracles, then we ended with the Lord's Prayer.

Thus fortified, we went inside and miracles unfolded before us. *Miracle Number One*: Although Nels had become unemployed two months earlier, his insurance was still in effect. If his heart attack had occurred four days later, he wouldn't have been covered. *Miracle Number Two*: We learned that Nels had filled out a form canceling that insurance. Argh! But he hadn't mailed it because he couldn't find a stamp. *Miracle Number Three*: We visited the local VA Hospital, where a sympathetic agent told us that because Nels had a still-unhealed skin lesion from the Vietnam War, he was qualified for full VA coverage for all conditions. Hallelujah! Meg filled out a mountain of paperwork, then the two us went back to my car, laughed with joy, held hands, and fervently thanked God for such a day of miracles.

WHY PRAY WITH AND FOR A COMPANION?

Prayer is part of our walk with God. We do it to grow in holiness, and praying with a spiritual companion helps us with our journey. It's a powerful way to experience God not as a distant deity, but rather as One who loves us with an eternal, no-matter-what, always and ever, unconditional love.

Shared prayer also bonds us together and helps us know one another's care at a felt level. Meg and I had been companions before Nels's medical crisis. We already had a spiritual and emotional connection. Praying together during the day of miracles deepened our bond and heightened our trust in one another. What a gift to have a friend we know we can call on when we have a pressing need, someone who's there for us, someone with a mutual love of God.

Another, more essential reason to pray: Spiritual companionship is both a human and a divine activity. Shared prayer allows God to be the center of the relationship and helps us sense his presence with us. That certainly was true for Meg and me during our day of miracles. Prayer ahead of time gave us an awareness of a quiet power that wasn't ours. We were more than a twosome. Together with God, we were a trio.

TWO FOUNDATIONS FOR SHARED PRAYER

Praying with a companion arises from a foundation of time spent alone with God, plus time with him through a faith community. They're like food and water. Without both of them we have little or nothing to offer each other. We'll end up trying to give from our emptiness, not from any fullness of God.

Meg's and my prayers would have been unlikely without each of us already having a one-on-one relationship with God. That's because when I pray for Meg, my prayers arise from my experiences of a Savior who is loving, humorous, inviting, trustworthy, strong, gentle. And Meg's prayers for me arise out of her own unique experiences of God. How could it be otherwise?

Then there's the foundation of the faith community and its importance. In the words of Father Ron Rolheiser,

> One of the central events that shaped Christian history, and history in general, happened not to an individual off praying alone or to a monk on a mountaintop. Pentecost happened at a meeting and it happened to a community, to a church congregation assembled for prayer, to a family of faith gathered to wait for God's guidance. It can be helpful to remember that. Our search for God should take us not just into private places of quiet and contemplation but, equally, into meeting rooms.[1]

Faith communities bring us into contact with people who cover the spectrum of young and old, conservatives and liberals, laity and ordained, the saintly and the not so saintly. Diversity doesn't allow us to get into a holy rut that excludes the world and the wider Body of Christ. Smugness becomes less likely because we encounter so much variety in others, so many opportunities to be less rigid, more humble; less closed, more open.

WHEN TO PRAY

"Pray without ceasing." So wrote Paul to the Thessalonians (1 Thess 5:17). Early in my enthusiasm for God, I took those words literally and tried praying nonstop for about a week. It wore me out. "A good ol' girl needs some time to herself," I finally groused, and gave it up. Later, those words "without ceasing" evolved into God often being on my mind in an almost subconscious way—not front and center but simply...there. Beyond personal prayer times and shared worship, now I frequently turn to God in thanksgiving or in need.

119

When do spiritual companions pray? They pray with and for each other during get-togethers. They also pray between sessions. For instance, after Meg's and my day of miracles, my prayers for her and Nels continued during personal prayer times. I prayed for God to guide and protect this couple. I prayed for strength for Meg, for wisdom for the medical people, for Nels's recovery. Later, I prayed in gratitude for how quickly he got well. I prayed for all this and more because I cared for these people and because Meg and I were committed to praying for one another. It was part of our spiritual companion relationship.

When Meg and I meet, we pray briefly at the start in order to transition into the session. It enables us to leave behind the outside world, especially helpful if we've been dealing with traffic snarls, difficult people, or nonstop news.

Briefly praying at the start also helps us become aware of God's presence and why we're meeting. This naturally flows into sharing what's going on in each of our lives. That, in turn, sets the stage for a key element in the companion relationship: praying together for each other's needs. I pray for Meg, then we switch and she prays for me. Each of us receives prayer for what was on her heart and mind when we arrived for our get-together. (Another option: some companions focus on one person per session.)

At the end of a session, Meg and I debrief what we've experienced. Then we close with a short prayer, perhaps thanking God for our time together, asking for protection on our journey home, blessings for our loved ones—in other words, whatever we feel like saying to God.

WHAT TO PRAY FOR

Companions pray as a follow-up to whatever each person has just shared. That can be a problem if, for instance, sharing time was spent talking about local news or showing each other the latest family photos. It takes self-discipline to concentrate on one another's spiritual life instead of other matters.

During prayer, companions focus on something they've brought with them to their session. It might be worry about a loved one, concern about an illness, wrestling with an important decision—anything. The goal is to draw closer to the One who cares about whatever is on each companion's heart and mind.

When Meg and I sit down to pray, she always asks me what I would like to pray about, and I do likewise with her. We do not presume to decide for the other person. Nor do we forget why we're praying: *The goal of the prayer time is to help one another experience God meeting us in our need.*

After Nels's heart attack, Meg often brought concerns about his recovery. We would pray about him for a little while, then shift the focus onto Meg. Why? Because Nels wasn't the one in the room during our sessions. Meg was. She needed inner strength to deal with her husband's illness. She needed hope. I had joined her during that day of miracles. Now the two of us prayed for God to give her a sense of his presence during Nels's recovery.

After praying for one companion, the focus turns to the other person so that each one's needs get met. As mentioned in chapter 9, "Sharing with a Companion," during the months before the 2016 presidential elections and the chaotic months that followed, I often felt so stressed that I couldn't sleep. Migraine headaches flattened me. Worry took over my life. So I would bring this to Meg's and my sessions and we would pray.

Those are two examples of a near infinity of what companions might pray for when they meet. Now comes a bigger challenge: how to pray.

"LORD, TEACH US TO PRAY" (LUKE 11:1)

For thousands of years people have worked on, struggled with, and asked themselves one question: How should we pray? The disciples asked Jesus to teach them, and he gave them the Lord's Prayer, rich and profound. I say it daily, but as with all prayer, it isn't a formula.

There is no formula for prayer, whether we're alone or with a spiritual companion. If there were a formula, it would be easy: do this; do that; say this; say that. Instead, we need sensitivity to the Holy Spirit. For prayer to be effective and life-giving, it must fit individuals and their situations.

Whatever style of prayer we prefer, it's important to speak directly to God. I sometimes hear someone say, "I want to ask God for...," or, "I want to thank God for...." That's addressing a group or a companion. It puts God at arm's length when what he longs for is a deep, you/me relationship with each of us. And so we pray, "Lord, *I* ask *you* for...," or, "Thank *you*, God, for...."

Praying together doesn't have to be out loud. I have a friend, a very effective pray-er, who always prays silently. She once said, "Praying out loud would be torture for me." However, after silently praying with her companion for awhile, she then says what she's sensed during prayer. She doesn't just pray and then say nothing, leaving her companion adrift to wonder what happened.

My friend's style matches what Meg and I do, except the two of us usually pray out loud to begin, then move into praying silently for a few minutes. Then we share what each of us has sensed within the silence. We often chat about that before going back into either silent or verbal prayer.

Because we both have unique issues, Meg and I don't blend our needs together. Instead, our prayer pattern focuses first on one of us then on the other. Pray, share, perhaps talk for a bit, then go back into prayer. Together, we dance with God.

Styles evolve. They also differ from companion to companion. I don't assume everyone is comfortable with the same prayer style I prefer. But regardless of a particular style, there is one constant to keep in mind: *Effective, powerful prayer is always based on love and acceptance.*

Acceptance includes warts and all, and sometimes those warts can be rather...warty. That, in turn, may give rise to several common prayer temptations:

1. *A temptation to offer advice.* This can occur in the midst of prayer or shortly afterward. However, no one can fix another person, even when a solution seems obvious. When tempted to offer advice to our companion, the words of Jesus can remind us of why we're praying: "Love one another. Just as I have loved you, you also should love one another" (John 13:34). In other words, Jesus urges us to love one another *in the same way* he loves each of us: unconditionally. This is far more effective than advice because love helps people experience God's presence with them, a presence that brings healing, strength, and spiritual growth—and isn't that the goal?

2. *A temptation to moralize.* During prayer, this might take the form of scripture. Let's imagine a man named Ira, whose companion, Al, might pray, "Oh God, we know that in 2 Thessalonians 3, Paul says some people are living lazy lives. I ask you, Lord, to heal Ira of his laziness. Help him see the error of his ways." Does Al actually say that? No. Why not? Because it wouldn't be loving. Instead of helping Ira draw closer to God, it probably would make him feel guilty and draw back in order to protect himself.

3. *A temptation to move beyond the limits of what our companion requests.* Here are Al and Ira again. Ira wants prayer for worry about his job. During prayer he tentatively hands his concern over to God. It would be inappropriate for Al to pray that Ira also hand his whole life over to God. That would be going ahead of where Ira currently is. It could cause him to panic and emotionally shut down.

Now for a common question: What specific prayers might we use when praying for one another? Answer: often the same ones we use when we're alone. Chapter 8 describes seven possibilities. Regardless of the prayers we choose, we never come to God as his equal. We always come as people in need of grace, mercy, and help. Often our prayers take the form of petition (praying for myself) and/or intercession (praying for others). What follows is how those might take shape with a spiritual companion.

First, with or without our awareness, God is always present—here in the room with us, loving us completely. He isn't a distant God who comes down to rescue us after we've said just the right words. So when we sit down to pray with our companion, the question isn't, Where is God? He's already here. The question is, What do we want to say to him? What is our need?

That was Meg's and my question at the start of our miracle day. Not knowing how to pray for so many needs, we began with one word: "Help!" We sat with a shared sense of neediness for a short while, then told God we were handing everything over to him. From this arose a prayer for an outpouring of the Spirit on everyone we'd meet that day.

Simply sharing a sense of neediness, as Meg and I did, can help us experience God's presence with us. A specific prayer request often follows. When nothing comes to mind, we might pray for God's enveloping love to surround the situation and the people involved in it. Or we can ask for a blessing on everyone. Still blank? All is not lost. Saint Paul says the Spirit remains with us, praying with and for us when we cannot do it ourselves:

> Likewise the Spirit helps us in our weakness; for we do not know how to pray as we ought, but that very Spirit intercedes with sighs too deep for words. And God, who searches the heart, knows what is the mind of the Spirit, because the Spirit intercedes for the saints according to the will of God. (Rom 8:26–27)

We can also pray for one another between sessions. Our prayers may be for our companions and the situations they care about, or they may be for anyone or anything else. This is a blessing of love and support that transcends miles and other limits. For instance, when I had major surgery in 2001, people said they'd be praying for me. And they did. During my recovery, I felt like I was lying in a hammock of prayer, and God's strength was pouring into me through people's prayers. What a gift—so effective yet unavailable for purchase in a pharmacy. Priceless.[2]

When praying with or for a companion, I've noticed two basic preferences that people have. Some like to focus on a need and pray for solutions. This is a problem-centered focus. But problems change from day to day. So even the finest prayers are likely to help only with that particular need. Often there's little or no carryover into solutions to new problems that inevitably arise.

My preference: envision myself or my companion interacting with God about a need. Where is God in this difficulty? Where am I (or my companion) with God? This style of prayer impacts many situations, not just one, because it leads to spiritual growth and empowerment. It keeps the focus in the room where we're gathered, not on some distant, problem-laden place.

Let's return to Ira and Al. Ira's job is at risk. He and Al can focus on the workplace or his boss. That might or might not bring the results they want. Instead of doing that, the two of them imagine Jesus being present with them. Ira prays, "Lord, my boss is such a perfectionist that it makes me too nervous to do my work. It's like I'm paralyzed. How will my family survive if I get laid off?"

After a few minutes, Ira relaxes a bit and imagines he's placing his problem into Jesus's hands. He and Al pray silently, then share what they experienced during that silence. Al says he had a mental picture of Jesus going to work with Ira each day and helping him do well. Ira says, "I sensed that production pressure at work is so high that my boss is worried about his own job. Maybe that's why he's giving everyone—not just me—such a hard time." Ira and Al briefly pray for the boss. Afterward Ira says he feels a bit sorry for him because he has a tough job. Ira also gets a sense of being cared for, regardless of what occurs. Anger and fear have been replaced by greater understanding and peace.

The two companions then turn their attention onto Al and his needs. After that, they close their time together with a prayer of thanksgiving for all that has happened during their session.

I often use words from scripture to speak with God and, through scripture, God speaks to me. I've underlined favorite passages in my Bible and turn to them for inspiration or solace or simply for an awareness of God's presence. It's a message that appears over and over in the Bible: "Have no fear,...says the LORD, for I am with you" (Jer 46:28a).

Scripture blesses us during personal prayer times and in companion sessions as well. Here are Ira and Al again: When praying together about Ira's job, Al recalls a passage from

Haggai, where God speaks to the Jews who felt too overwhelmed to rebuild their temple in Jerusalem. Instead of using the original name in Haggai (Zerubbabel), Al substitutes Ira's: "Now take courage, Ira, says the LORD; work, for I am with you, says the LORD of hosts. My spirit abides among you; do not fear" (see Hag 2:4–5).

Scripture includes a style of prayer that Saint Paul specialized in: the prayer of affirmation. He loved the people he ministered to and affirmed them when he wrote to their communities: "We always give thanks to God for all of you and mention you in our prayers, constantly remembering before our God and Father your work of faith and labor of love" (1 Thess 1:2–3a).

Faith and hard work: Saint Paul saw those gifts and thanked God for them. Then he went beyond that by telling faith communities what he saw. He didn't keep his gratitude to himself. Instead, he affirmed people whose many challenges included persecution and the uncertainties of how to live out a new faith.

As noted in chapter 5, when using affirmation during prayer, we openly express gratitude to God for what we see in our companion—some strength, some virtue, some goodness. We see our companions as God sees them and that, in turn, helps them see themselves the same way.

Scripture, affirmation, petition, and intercession are just a few ways to pray with and for a companion. Another favorite of mine: praying with music. Meg and I often start with this after we're done sharing and are sitting down to pray. We might put on music from a monastery and listen to a contemplative hymn. Or we may sing a simple hymn we both know such as the "Eightfold Alleluia." Singing the same words and breathing together unites us and helps us know that God is with us. Whatever form it takes, music is a beautiful way to transition into the prayer phase of a companion session.

Finally, Christianity's overflowing treasure chest of prayers contains traditional, memorized ones. These are great for a closing prayer for any gathering, including gathering with our companion. Meg and I sometimes close with the Lord's Prayer. Or we may end our session with yet another type of prayer: a prayer of thanksgiving for all that has happened during our time together, all the blessings we have received.

CONCLUSION

My late coauthor, Father Leo Thomas, said prayer is the most important activity of spiritual companions. It's a powerful way for God's grace to flow through us to each other. But no matter how good we get at it, we'll never be prayer experts because we are finite creatures in relationship with our infinite God. This is OK. God does not expect us to be great prayers. He just wants us to keep turning to him in prayer, both as individuals and as companions. He invites us to trust our inner promptings, to trust him, to hear what he longs for each of us to know: "I love all your prayers. I love you."

FOR YOUR REFLECTION

1. Have you ever prayed for someone who wasn't with you—perhaps a sick relative or a friend going through a divorce? If yes, how did you pray? What kind(s) of prayers did you pray?
2. Have you ever prayed *with* someone—someone who was present? If yes, what was the experience like? (It

can be kind of scary or awkward at first.) How did you pray? Silently? Out loud? What type(s) of prayer did you use?

3. If you have a spiritual companion, do you pray together when you meet? If yes, when and how do you pray? If you typically don't pray when you meet, how might you begin to fit that into your sessions?

4. "The Lord is near. Do not worry about anything, but in everything by prayer and supplication with thanksgiving let your requests be made known to God. And the peace of God, which surpasses all understanding, will guard your hearts and your minds in Christ Jesus" (Phil 4:5b–7).

When the world around us or within us is in turmoil, prayer can ease our worries and give us inner peace. Praying with a companion is an especially powerful way for this to take place. I invite you to ponder the above words from Paul's letter to the Philippians and pray for the Holy Spirit to protect you from worry, to guard your heart and mind, and give you peace.

CHAPTER II

Reflecting on Experiences of God

IN THIS CHAPTER:

The importance of reflecting on our experiences

Recognizing experiences of God

Understanding an experience of God

Reflecting with a spiritual companion

> God so desires to be found that he is constantly clearing his throat.
>
> —Meister Eckhart

Several years ago, I took a AAA safe-driving class in order to lower my auto insurance by a pittance. With the exception of a few young adult males, attendees were—how shall I put this?—gray haired. Curious, I approached one of the twenty-something guys during a break and asked him why he was taking the class. "To lower the fine I got for speeding on I-405," he said.

"How fast were you going?" I asked.

"160."

This amazed me. Not the speed, but the fact that, given the traffic congestion on 405, it was possible to drive that fast on that road. But I believed him and asked my next question: "How big was your fine?"

Let me pause here and say that whenever I tell this story to others, I always ask them to guess the largest fine they can imagine. They never go high enough because his answer was...

"$8,000."

Before I could wrap my brain around this astonishing number, class reconvened, but at the end of the day, I sidled up to the young man and quietly said, "From now on, try to keep the speed below triple digits."

"Oh, don't worry!" he exclaimed. "I haven't gone over the speed limit since I got that ticket."

Here was someone who had an experience and was reflecting on it—probably less about the thrill of speeding and more on the pain of what came next. I hope his ticket helped him become a safer driver rather than cause him to look for ways to avoid detection.

Reflecting on our experiences is a path to growing in wisdom and in life skills. The general principle here is, *we learn and grow by reflecting on our life.*

Without reflection, mistakes get repeated again and again. We don't learn. We don't grow. The driver in my AAA class would keep pursuing the thrill of speeding. He'd get more tickets and possibly lose his license. He might even lose control of his car one day and lose his life. Tragic losses, so preventable.

It isn't just painful experiences that invite us to reflect on what has occurred. So do good ones. Without reflection, they're like happy accidents rather than opportunities. My chapter on affirmation describes how I used to give little thought to positive feedback about my writing. People's words felt good but they held no meaning until I received a cash award in a writing contest. Then I reflected on what it meant. From those reflections came an awareness that God had given me a gift of writing. This, in turn, led to a realization that God wanted me to develop the gift and use it for others.

Spiritual companions are a grace-filled tool for helping us reflect on what happens to us. They are like living mirrors. Just as we cannot know what we look like without a mirror, we cannot see ourselves clearly without other people's wisdom, insight, and support. Companions enable us to recognize what we otherwise might miss. They help us reflect so that thoughts don't go around and around inside our head on a mental merry-go-round.

RECOGNIZING AN EXPERIENCE OF GOD

I can't reflect on an experience if I don't realize I've had one. Some are hard to overlook, like an $8,000 traffic fine. Others are easy to miss, such as experiences of God. The Creator of the universe is like the air we breathe: present everywhere, essential for our moment-by-moment existence, yet seldom obvious. How can we become aware of his presence? Where should we seek? One place is in nature: "The heavens are telling the glory of God; and the firmament proclaims his handiwork....There is no speech, nor are there words; their voice is not heard; yet their voice goes out through all the earth, and their words to the end of the world" (Ps 19:1, 3–4).

This is like the story of a child who stood at a lakeshore with his grandfather one evening, watching a glorious, multicolored sunset. After a few minutes, the grandfather took off his hat, placed it over his heart, and said, "My son, it is the Lord."

Clearly this man saw beyond a sunset and recognized its Maker. He responded with an act of prayer: placing his hat over his heart. Like him, we can come to know and love the Creator of the universe through what lies before us every day: creation itself. Not only sunsets but also birds, flowers, forests, oceans, mountains—an infinity of beauty.

Just stepping outside can make us aware of God's presence and love for us. Many experiences are nondramatic, like the morning I was gardening and felt a warm, gentle breeze that seemed like the breath of God, so tender. It reminded me of the Old Testament account of Elijah when he was hiding in a cave for fear of his life. God told him he was going to appear to him, and Elijah expected high drama. Here's what happened instead:

> A great and powerful wind tore the mountains apart and shattered the rocks before the LORD, but the LORD was not in the wind. After the wind there was an earthquake, but the LORD was not in the earthquake. After the earthquake came a fire, but the LORD was not in the fire. And after the fire came a gentle whisper. When Elijah heard it, he pulled his cloak over his face and went out and stood at the mouth of the cave. (1 Kgs 19:11b–13, NIV)

This passage is an example of another way God communicates with us: through scripture, often called "the word of the Lord." It's a word written not just for scholars and saints but for each of us as well. Within its pages we read about God's never-failing love for us; his will for us; his call to grow and, yes, sometimes repent. Other people's experiences of him over the course of thousands of years can speak to us personally about our own lives.

Regardless of how God communicates with us, our ability to recognize that fact is impacted by human relationships, for better or for worse. Some people have had superb role models and learned loving things about God. Their spiritual antennae are more easily tuned to him because of their relationships.

However, if young people aren't taught anything about God, their ability to recognize his presence will be harmed. As children of God, each of us has a profound spiritual nature, but we aren't born automatically knowing who God is. If no one tells me about Jesus, I'm not going to wake up one day and say, "You know, I think a man named Jesus was born two thousand years ago...." Instead, I'll be religiously illiterate, like the five-year-old whose mother overheard a conversation between him and a neighbor boy. The woman told me the boy said something about God and her son said, "God? Who's that?"

An even bigger problem: Some people have heard distorted messages about God over the years—perhaps that he's a tyrant, or he gives children birth defects, or refuses salvation to sinners and sends them to hell. (Since all of us are sinners, this last fallacy presents particularly big problems.) It may take years for people to overcome distortions like these. They are like a poorly recorded CD. It needs to be recorded over by a beautiful one. Before that occurs, people may not *want* any experiences of God.

UNDERSTANDING EXPERIENCES OF GOD

Reflecting on life experiences—sunsets, traffic tickets, anything—is a powerful way to recognize God in them. But it's not enough to be aware of an experience of God. We also need to understand its meaning so we don't misinterpret it.

Take, for instance, Francis of Assisi in 1204. He'd gone from flamboyant party boy, to glory-seeking soldier, to prisoner of war in a dungeon, to ill and depressed veteran, then finally, to religious convert. One fall day he went to pray in a wreck of a little church in San Damiano. Suddenly overcome by a gaze of Jesus coming from a crucifix over the altar, Francis sensed the Lord saying to him, "Francis! Rebuild my church which, as you can see, has fallen in ruins."

An experience of God? Definitely. Understanding it? In Francis's case, not immediately. Looking around at the tumbledown building he was in, he concluded that God wanted him to repair it. So he spent the next three years begging in the streets for alms to rebuild the San Damiano church.

Enlightenment eventually dawned during a Mass in 1208. The gospel reading that day urged listeners to leave behind their riches then go forth to preach repentance to sinners and to announce the kingdom of God everywhere. With these words, something clicked in Francis's mind: God's call to him wasn't about a collapsed building. It was about a church in the need of reform and a world in need of healing.

Off Francis went in a new direction. The same zest he'd had as a young man now became an asset. He exuberantly spread the good news of Jesus Christ to everyone he met. His contagious joy attracted followers. "May the Lord give you peace," he'd always begin. He showed people the beauty and glory of God's creation. He preached salvation. He created the first nativity scene in order to make the Holy Family's poverty and vulnerability real to everyone. All of this from an initial experience of God, followed by understanding several years later, followed by a yes to God from a man whom the Catholic Church now calls the patron saint of ecology.[1]

No formula exists for understanding experiences of God. Awareness will vary from person to person because each of us filters events through who we are and what our life is and has already been. Here are several ways that can help us grow in understanding:

1. *Daily personal prayer.* For me, only a few of my experiences of God have been dramatic. Usually they're subtle. That's why I set aside about twenty minutes each morning to pray and reflect on what occurred during the past twenty-four hours. Often that's when the "ah-ha" moment comes. After the fact, I awaken to God's presence in what recently occurred. I'm like Jacob waking from a dream where he saw a stairway reaching to heaven: "Surely," he said afterward, "the LORD is in this place—and I did not know it!" (Gen 28:16).

   Private time with God gives us a chance to ponder; to pay attention to situations, feelings, and events; to think about where God might possibly be in them. Insights may come as we notice our feelings, inner promptings, inspirations, thoughts, hunches. In my case, these usually are easy to overlook unless I'm paying attention and expecting God to communicate with me through my thoughts and feelings.

   Given today's lifestyle habits—the ceaseless checking of cell phones and filling every waking minute with news, music, and text messages—making time to ponder anything may require an act of great willpower. It also may mean a polite refusal to meet others' expectations that we be available to them all day, every day. And night.

2. *Study of scripture.* Windows of my mind open up when I take a scripture class. Passages in the Bible that once confused me become clearer and sometimes give me an "ah-ha!" moment. A few passages challenge me—those I may not have understood or ones I've conveniently ignored.

For instance, I once took a class that focused on the Bible's teachings on living our faith. It covered passages like the Ten Commandments and the verse where Jesus says, "You shall love your neighbor as yourself" (Matt 22:39). At the end of the thirty-hour series, participants were invited to share one thing they had gained from the class. When my turn came, I stood up and said, "I've always known I was a sinner. Now I know the details." That class humbled me. It shook me out of complacency and increased my awareness of the needs of people both near and far.

3. *Hearing about others' experiences of God.* When people describe an experience about God or anything else, something they say may help us understand our own life. It may be a friend's life, or a saint's life, or a person in the Bible, or anyone. It can be a testimonial in church, an op-ed piece in a newspaper, a speaker. Other people's lives can help us become aware of God's presence in our own.

   For example, years ago I gave a talk based on a chapter in my book *Healing.* Called "From Good Friday to Pentecost and Beyond," it compares Jesus's journey (often called the paschal mystery) to our own journey through the stages of grief when we suffer a major loss. Afterward, a woman came up to me and said, "My husband died two years ago. This is the first time that my life since then has made any sense to me." A man told me essentially the same thing, only in his case he'd been in an auto accident a year earlier and now was too disabled to work. Naming what he was going through helped him feel less confused, less alone, and closer to God.

4. *Sharing with spiritual companions.* Companions help us interpret the meaning of events, feelings, situations, or

137

in the case of Francis of Assisi, messages from God. So I wonder: If he had had a spiritual companion when he heard Jesus's call to rebuild a ruined church, would it have taken him three years to understand it? He had an experience of God but lacked an understanding of its meaning and deeper call. That's what a spiritual companion could have helped him do: bring his experience into clearer focus and reveal its deeper truth.

Alone, the human brain can zing off in an odd direction, not unlike Francis's initial response to Jesus's message. He immediately went to his father's fabric shop, helped himself to its finest cloth, sold it, and gave the money to the priest in charge of the San Damiano church. When the obvious was pointed out to him by his irate father—the cloth belonged to him— Francis retrieved the money and returned it. Then he renounced all his possessions, even going so far as to strip off his clothes in the public square, hand them to his father, and stand buck naked in front of a startled crowd that included the local bishop. From there he went forth in borrowed rags to beg for funds for the little church in San Damiano.

If I had been Francis's spiritual companion in 1204, the first thing I'd do after witnessing his sensational behavior would be to stifle my desire to say, "Are you *nuts*?" Instead, after calming myself and centering my mind on God, I might say, "Wait, let's talk about this. Tell me what Jesus said." This could lead to looking at, and praying about, what "ruined church" meant to Francis and, more importantly, to God.

REFLECTING WITH A
SPIRITUAL COMPANION

Sharing and praying with companions can help us discern which experiences are from the Lord and which ones are simply our own thoughts or feelings. Personally, I rarely have earth-shaking experiences of God. Most of mine are subtle and arise from what's occurring around me and within me at the moment. What a blessing to have someone with whom I can share them!

In addition to confirming experiences of God, companions encourage us to respond. This often happens through affirmation and listening, both of which bring out the best in us and strengthen us to say yes to God's call. "Yes" is not an automatic response, because questions and feelings naturally arise when faced with something unexpected or new. Here are a few examples from scripture:

1. *Isaiah* has a vision of the Lord seated on a throne. Reaction: "Woe is me! I am lost, for I am a man of unclean lips…yet my eyes have seen the King, the LORD of hosts!" But after his lips are cleansed by an angel, he says, "Here am I; send me!" when God asks who will go speak for him to the Israelites (Isa 6:1–8).

2. *Mary* is troubled when an angel appears and tells her she will conceive a child who will be called "Son of the Most High." Reaction: "How can this be, since I am a virgin?" Then after being reassured, she says, "Here am I, the servant of the Lord; let it be with me according to your word" (Luke 1:26–38).

3. *The rich young man* asks Jesus what he must do to inherit eternal life. Jesus invites him to follow him after the young man sells his possessions and gives

139

his money to the poor. Reaction: Turns down the invitation. Walks away sad (Matt 19:16–22).

4. *Peter* is astonished when he catches a massive number of fish after obeying Jesus's instructions to put out his nets. Reaction: Falls to his knees and says, "Go away from me, Lord, for I am a sinful man!" After Jesus says, "Do not be afraid; from now on you will be catching people," Peter and his partners, James and John, leave everything and follow Jesus (Luke 5:1–11).

Let us move now from the lofty (scripture) to the practical (a companion session). Since Jesus is part of the relationship, including him makes sense. Here are some ideas for reflecting together, questions that companions might ask each other. Answers can be an excellent lead-in to praying together afterward.

1. *How do you experience God when you pray?* A good general question, especially when people are in the early stages of being companions.

2. Another good question early on in a companion relationship: *How do you "imagine" God?* For example: Savior? Friend? Breath/Ruah? Judge? All-controlling? It also can be helpful for particular situations because our thoughts about God can vary according to what is occurring.

3. *How do you think God sees you? What age are you in his eyes?* Odd questions, perhaps, but the answer can help clarify expectations we have of ourselves.

4. In response to a companion's description of a situation/event: *Do you sense God in this?* Or perhaps: *How do you sense God in this? What do you hear him saying to you?* These questions often startle people. God? In this situation? It's a new thought that can cause them to shift mental gears and open themselves to consciously bring God into something that's happening.

CONCLUSION

If we only recognize God in ultra-clear, dramatic experiences, we may think we rarely hear from him. Other people experience the Lord often, but not us. Other people are more holy or more blessed than we are. Not true. Most experiences of God come to us like love itself—gently, quietly, inviting a response. They weave themselves into our life until they become part of who we are. Let us pray for the grace to say yes to this great love, yes to God.

FOR YOUR REFLECTION

1. This chapter includes four questions companions might ask each other. Before asking those questions of someone else, ask them for yourself during time alone with God. What are your thoughts or feelings about them?
   a. How do you experience God when you pray?
   b. How do you "imagine" God?
   c. How do you think God sees you? What age are you in his eyes?
   d. Reflect on a situation or event that has occurred in your life: Did you sense God in this, or perhaps, *how* did you sense God in this? What did you hear him saying to you?
2. Have you ever had an "ah-ha!" moment after telling someone about an experience you had? Some breakthrough in understanding after this person listened to you? What was that like? How important was it to you in your spiritual journey?

SEEKING *Christ* THROUGH *Friendship*

3. Has anyone ever had an "ah-ha!" moment after you were the one in the role of listener? What was that experience like for you?
4. In closing, a prayer:

Lord, I ask you to give me eyes to see, ears to hear, and senses to feel your presence. Help me know—somehow, someway—that you truly are with me always. Amen.

CHAPTER 12

Discernment

IN THIS CHAPTER:

What is discernment?

Two views of God's will

Seeking God's will

The discernment process

Four items that need to fit together

Decisions, decisions

If I take the wings of the morning
    and settle at the farthest limits of the sea,
even there your hand shall lead me.
                                    —Psalm 139:9–10a

INTRODUCTION

Years ago, I drove a homeless man to a shelter after attending a prayer meeting. Then I got lost. Driving aimlessly in a deserted industrial area of Seattle, I kept making wrong turns in my search for a northbound freeway ramp. Every choice on that dark night led to more confusion. Finally, I got mad and complained to God about this state of affairs. "Lord," I said, "I just did a good deed and now I'm lost. Help me find this blasted entrance!"

I said this while sitting at an intersection, waiting for a red light to change. As soon as my words left my lips, I got a sense of Jesus behind me in the back seat, leaning forward and calmly saying, "Turn left."

Did I instantly follow his direction? I did not. Instead, I argued: "Here? That makes no sense." But then I thought, *Wait a minute, Jan. If God is the one giving you these directions, maybe he knows what he's talking about. Maybe you should turn left, now.* So I did. Two blocks later, there was the road I'd been seeking for twenty minutes. And two blocks after that, there was that elusive freeway ramp.

There are times in my life when I sit at a different kind of intersection, a decision-making point about my career or volunteer work or finances or a zillion other issues. Options lie before me: this or that; yes or no; go or stay. My mind bounces back and forth like a tennis ball at Wimbledon. Anxiety rises as I worry about making the wrong choice. What to do, what to do....Ah, here's a way out: let God choose for me. So I ask. I want God to say, "Do this, not that." Alas, he rarely does. So instead, I enter into a more challenging, yet life-giving process called discernment.

WHAT IS DISCERNMENT?

Look up this word in a dictionary and it will say something about detecting by sight or senses, coming to know or recognize or see clearly. When it comes to God and us, what comes to mind for me is a prayer that Saint Richard of Chichester prayed when he was near death in 1253: "O most merciful redeemer, friend and brother, may I know thee more clearly, love thee more dearly, and follow thee more nearly, day by day. Amen."

Saint Richard's first request isn't to follow Christ. Instead, he starts by asking God to help him "know thee more clearly"—to sense God's presence and be in relationship with him. After that comes falling in love and then, finally, following God more closely every day.

Eight hundred years later, the same prayer can empower us: knowing God at a felt level and loving him leads to our wanting to include him in the myriad choices we make about our lives. We pray for discernment, for the grace to take paths that will draw us closer to the Lord and to humankind.

Discernment involves choosing between two (or more) options, each of them basically good. I don't wake up one morning and fret about whether to rob a bank that day, or have an affair, or falsify my income taxes. Two of those are crimes, all of them are sins, and God never invites us to sin. That leaves us, then, with choosing the good and seeking God's will about which is the best one at this time. How we look upon that process depends on our thoughts about God's will. What follows are two basic viewpoints.

TWO VIEWS OF GOD'S WILL

One viewpoint looks upon God's will as a divine blueprint—a predetermined road map for our lives. Our job is to discover our destiny. This can make us anxious because we're hunting for an already-devised plan that's hidden who knows where. And if we fail to discover it? God is not happy. We're not happy. We had our chance and muffed it.

A road map perspective often causes fear and insecurity. To avoid that, people may seek whatever makes them feel safe— things like infallible prescriptions, or legalisms such as laws, rules, or certain scripture passages. Some join cults that take over their free will for them; blindly following someone in authority removes the burden of being responsible for their own actions.

A predetermined viewpoint may also tempt people to use magic, to look for "signs" in places like horoscopes. Some play "Bible roulette," where they close their eyes, open a Bible, put their finger down on a page, then read what verse their finger is pointing to. That's God's will for them. OK, I some-times do this in a modified way: I randomly page through my Bible to see if anything resonates with what I'm going through at the moment. I don't use this as a tool for discern-ment but rather as a way to connect my own life with the life I find in scripture.

The second view of God's will focuses on his goals, on what he wants for us and for the world. Jesus made this very clear in the Gospel of John: "I came that they may have life, and have it abundantly." (10:10b). God doesn't give us a map or a GPS route. ("Turn left in one mile.") Instead, he invites us to join him on a daily spiritual journey where we already know what God wants: abundant life for ourselves and others. Regardless of where we started out or where we are now, God offers us many choices for arriving at our destination.

That sounds liberating, but here's the challenge: to make God's goals ours as well—to be mature, free, loving children of God; to have faith, hope, and love be our basic values instead of those that surround us each day: wealth, power, prestige, media distractions. What—and whose—values will we seek?

146

SEEKING GOD'S WILL

God invites us to live as his children and be part of the great design he has for the world. Being part of that design periodically brings us to a crossroad where we might, or might not, seek God's input. Some people do, others shy away from wanting to know what God wants.

For example, let us imagine a young man named Brad. He's a senior in high school who has been hearing a question that every child hears ad nauseum: "What do you want to be when you grow up?" He isn't sure, but he does know one thing: his father owns a butcher shop and expects Brad to take over ownership of it when he retires. Brad often works there after school and has discovered that this isn't the life he wants. And besides, being surrounded by meat every day has led him to secretly long to be (gasp!) a vegetarian.

Brad knows a bit about God and half-heartedly prays about what to do after graduation. But he doesn't really want to get an answer because he doesn't want God, or his father or anyone else, telling him what to do. Instead, he wants his heart's desire, whatever that turns out to be.

In this story, we see a common mistake: a belief that what God wants for us probably differs from what we want. So if we seek God's will when we're at a decision-making point, he'll tell us to do something we really don't want to do, like take over ownership of a butcher shop.

Scripture tells us we are temples of the Holy Spirit (1 Cor 6:19). When we search within, down to our most authentic self, that's where we discover the Spirit. That's also where we discover our deepest desires, ones that may differ from what we thought we wanted. In other words, God wants what we want. Our desires have been given to us as part of the unique person God created us to be.

This good news is not without its problems. For one thing, it's easy to confuse superficial desires with deeper, more authentic ones. It's also easy to buy into what other people want—"shoulds" from society or loved ones like Brad's father. Here is where a discernment process can help us avoid rash decisions that lead us away from choices that will lead to the abundant life we long for.

THE DISCERNMENT PROCESS

Typically, discernment gradually unfolds. But occasionally God acts dramatically with a clear sign, saying, "Here is my plan for you. Will you say yes?"

The Gospel of Luke describes that type of event in the life of Mary, a teenager engaged to a carpenter named Joseph. She's living an ordinary life in a nothing town in a barely something country, when a divine messenger suddenly appears with shocking news: God's plan is for her to be the mother of the Messiah. Mary, not surprisingly, is surprised, especially since she's a virgin. The angel explains more, then it's Mary's turn. What is her answer? Christians down through the ages have celebrated her yes (Luke 1:38).

In our own life, even when a sign seems to point to God as its source, it's important to confirm that it's the Lord who is acting, speaking, or calling. Then our only decision is yes or no. In Mary's case, the angel confirmed the validity of God's message by telling her about a hopeless situation that no longer was hopeless: "Your relative Elizabeth in her old age has also conceived a son....For nothing will be impossible with God" (Luke 1:36–37).

A spiritual companion can help us confirm that an experience we've had is from the Lord, that God is acting in our life and offering us an opportunity. But if a decision will impact other people such as family members, it's important to include them as well, to not leave them out of the picture.

We have free will. We can say no. Even Mary could have turned down God's invitation to become the mother of the Messiah. But with a call from God comes the grace for us to say yes. We receive courage and strength. I greatly admire Mary for her yes. She had no way of knowing if Joseph would still want to marry her when he found out he wasn't the father of this child. Worse yet, being pregnant out of wedlock at that time was a capital crime. In agreeing to God's plan, Mary risked being stoned to death.

Dramatic messages from God are rare. So what do we do when a decision lies before us and no angel appears? Sometimes a profound sense of rightness and peace will settle over us. In cases like that, we don't need to go through a lengthy discernment process. We simply know deep down what our calling from God is at this time.

For example, eighteen months after Fred and I married, I gave birth to identical twin girls, beautiful four-pound preemies who needed a lot of care for a lot of months. (Me to Fred, when I sometimes needed help at 2:00 a.m.: "Do you want to feed one baby now, or two babies and one wife tomorrow?")

The best I can say about those days is, the four of us survived. When the fog of exhaustion finally lifted, Fred and I pondered the possibility of my returning to work as a physical therapist. But no relatives lived within two thousand miles, and we would have no backup plan for anything unexpected. We calculated that by being frugal, frugal, frugal, we could make it on one salary. One decision seemed logical and totally right for our situation: I would be a stay-at-home mother for the first six years of our daughters' lives. After that? We'd see.

A spiritual companion can help us confirm our sense of rightness and trust its accuracy. Here again, it's important to include family members who will be impacted by our decision. In my case, Fred's thinking matched mine as well.

What do we do when there's been no dramatic act on God's part, and when we have no profound sense of rightness? What do we do when all we hear is the sound of silence? That's the usual situation. When (not if) that happens, I recommend a three-step discernment process developed by Saint Ignatius of Loyola.

Step One: Pray for Freedom and Guidance

Right from the start, we include God in our decision-making. He's the first resort, not the last—not the One we turn to for a seal of approval after we've already decided what we want.

Praying for freedom and guidance doesn't mean a onetime Our Father and then we check off that item. Instead, prayer occurs throughout the entire journey toward a significant decision.

- We pray to be free from undue influences, either external (from other people) or internal (superficial "wants" rather than deep longings).
- We pray that our primary focus is toward God.
- We pray for whatever guidance we need so our choice is made using Christian values.

For example, when our daughters were born, Fred and I had a profound sense of rightness that I be a stay-at-home mother until the girls were six. When they entered school, I revisited the earlier decision. Remain at home or return to work? I began praying, every day, for months. This was the 1970s, a time when society frowned upon women who chose full-time motherhood. Daily prayer helped me ignore subtle and sometimes overt messages from acquaintances and the media that said I should return to work. Instead, I asked God what he wanted for the family and for me. I knew I had more time now and was being called to some kind of work, but what was it?

Spiritual companions can be a wonderful resource during step 1. Simply sitting down and praying together helps still the voices of the outside world. It keeps the focus on God. This is not the time for answers. It's just a time for focusing on God and asking for guidance.

Step Two: Prayerfully Use Your Reasoning

Saint Ignatius promoted reasoning as one way to turn on our spiritual antennae. He suggested that it include a list. First, we list negatives of a decision, then positives. Looking at cons before pros may help us avoid a natural temptation to do a sales job on one choice or the other—often the positive side. Instead, we adopt an attitude of what Ignatius called "holy indifference," which I prefer to call "holy neutrality." We can go either way with a choice. We're neutral. Our focus is on what God wants, trusting that that also, deep down, is what we want. At times like this, I pray, "Lord, I want what you want."

This was my prayer during one of several periods when I revisited earlier decisions to be a stay-at-home mom. Here were a few items on my list:

Negatives of working outside the home:
- Dealing with childcare during the hours and days when the girls weren't in school.
- Childcare costs. I would need a fairly significant salary to offset it.
- I now had a chronic illness that sometimes flared up and flattened me.

Positives:

- Working as a PT would bring in added income and remove the insecurity that came from being a single-income household.
- Outside work would be mentally and socially stimulating. Being home full time sometimes felt like an IQ-lowering lifestyle.

Reasoning may start with a list, but it doesn't end there. Now it's important to mentally, emotionally, and spiritually live with our options. Like trying on shoes before buying a pair, we try on alternatives to see how each one "fits" or feels. It helps to do this for awhile, to allow at least a week per option.

For me, the trying-on process included several visits to a PT department to observe patient care. One day I chatted with a patient being treated for neck pain. After a few minutes she told me about a problem she was having: "My husband sleeps through any alarm, so it's my job to wake him up in time for work, but I'm a heavy sleeper too, so every night I sleep sitting up in a kitchen chair because if I don't, he'll be late and get fired and it'll be my fault."

I stared in amazement at this woman, who probably looked like a bobblehead as she slept upright each night. She didn't need treatment for neck pain, of which the cause was fairly obvious. She needed marriage counseling. With that thought came another one, crystal clear: I wanted to help people whose needs were deeper than physical. I didn't know what this meant. I only knew it wasn't PT.

During step 2, spiritual companions chat, share a decision's pros and cons, listen and listen some more, ask questions, and reflect statements back to one another. Each of us is a safety net, helping our companion avoid outside pressure or rash decisions. The goal is to move beneath superficial desires, to get in touch with deeper ones and sense God's presence. Therefore we *don't* give advice or voice opinions to our companion—a natural temptation at this stage. Instead, we are a divine presence.

Step Three: Seek Confirmation in Peace

In any important decision, we need what Saint Ignatius called "discernment of spirits,"[1] a process that assumes God communicates directly with us through our feelings, thoughts, and desires. We want a decision to come from God, but that's not a given. Instead, it might arise from fear or a desire to please others, or from some other source. This is why step 3 is so important: It's when we ask God to bless a decision if it is his will. We also ask him to somehow let us know if it isn't.

Confirmation includes a personal sense of "rightness" about a decision. As with the other two steps, prayer is essential so that we don't act on the basis of a mood. We also don't want a decision to come from a feeling of relief that may arise because we've made a choice. That back-and-forth, yes-or-no torment finally is over, we think. Who cares if we've made the best decision? Well, God cares, and ultimately we'll care too if we end up feeling caught in a trap of our own making.

A sense of peace also isn't the same as escapism, a temptation that may arise in a stressful situation. For instance, a father of three children under the age of four, one of whom has colic and keeps him up walking the floor with her each night, may suddenly believe he's called to become a celibate priest. Now. Of course not. What this man needs is a break and outside help, not a career change. His wife undoubtedly needs the same thing.

The personal peace we seek in step 3 won't occur without acceptance of consequences: every decision costs us something. Some suffering is inevitable. When my daughters were teenagers, I often chanted a mantra: "You pay a price for every decision you make, even positive ones." In their case at that age, it was study now and go to college later; or play now, flunk courses, and later pay a steep price of no college.

For the ultimate example of paying a steep price, we need look no further than Jesus in the Garden of Gethsemane. He could have fled that night but chose not to. Instead, he chose love and paid for that decision with his life. But look at the outcome: eternal life for us.

My decision to give up a physical therapy career cost Fred and me a second income. However, it created space for new paths. I never dreamed it would lead to healing ministry, writing, and cocreating a priest's legacy. God was full of surprises. Those surprises unfolded over a period of years, and spiritual companions joined me during each one. In step 3, their basic role was to confirm a sense of rightness I might be having or invite me to rethink it.

FOUR ITEMS THAT NEED TO FIT TOGETHER

During times of discernment, I look at four items that should fit together:

1. *Scripture and the teachings of our faith community.* Does a decision stay within these boundaries? This assumes we're familiar enough with scripture and connected closely enough to a faith community to know what is and isn't wise from both perspectives.

But what if....What if some past decisions were unwise or even sinful? What if we made poor decisions in the past that still impact us today? Jesus addresses this issue in his parable about the prodigal son (Luke 15:11–32).

This is the story of a young man who one day says to his father, "Give me the share of the property that will belong to me" (15:12). Since property back then didn't come to offspring until their father died, the son is basically saying, "Dad, I wish you were dead." But no matter. The father gives him his share and a few days later he goes off and sinks into over-the-top hedonism.

Eventually, the mantra I chanted to my daughters comes to pass for this man because when he runs out of money, his decision costs him dearly. He ends up working at a job that would be a horror for any Jew: feeding pigs. This ultimate, in-the-gutter degradation finally awakens him to a better option: go home, tell his dad he has sinned, and ask to work for him as a servant. So he goes.

The father welcomes his son with open arms and celebrates his return, and that's what Jesus wants us to know: his Father is like that father. God watches and waits for us with loving anticipation. No matter how poor our choices may have been in the past, he welcomes us and assures us that all is not lost. He has a positive future in mind for us.

"I know the plans I have for you, says the LORD, plans for your welfare and not for harm, to give you a future with hope. Then when you call upon me and come and pray to me, I will hear you. When you search for me, you will find me" (Jer 29:11–13).

I don't believe the above promise would be possible if God had only one plan for each of us. Instead, God takes every choice we make and uses it to create a hope-filled future. Here's how my spiritual director, Father Jack, once described it with enthusiasm: "I think God's creativity is infinite! It's like he has this incredible, giant computer that can develop a new plan every minute. Whatever choice I make or whatever happens to me, God creates a plan that can fit into that."

In other words, even if we've lived a prodigal son life or suffered heartbreaking tragedies, all is not lost. God can and does bring good out of bad. I find this consoling about the past and liberating for the future of my own life and the lives of others.

SEEKING *Christ* THROUGH *Friendship*

2. *Community input.* Community input is essential because if we want something badly enough, we can fool ourselves into believing that not only do we want it, so does God. A little red flag goes up in my head whenever I hear someone say, "God told me to do this." Sometimes God did, but sometimes it turns out that he didn't. In those cases, community input can save us from pain, embarrassment, false starts, and wrong turns.

No one individual is our whole community, not even a spiritual companion. Yes, a companion is a great gift during a discernment process, but two people, by themselves, don't do as well as two people who belong to a larger faith community.

Community also includes our immediate family. Fred was a vital part of my decision to close the door on physical therapy. If he had thought it unwise, I would have reconsidered what I thought was final.

3. *Personal circumstances.* Personal circumstances play a big part in the plans God has in mind for each of us. Looking at options reminds me of our home's main hallway. It's fourteen feet long, four feet wide, with eight doors opening into it. When I'm in the midst of making a major decision, it's as if each possibility is a door, and I'm free to try it. But when I do that, I discover that some doors aren't just closed; they're locked. Others can be opened, but I don't like what I see when I step inside and look around.

Ah, but now comes that eighth door. It's not only unlocked, it's wide open. And there's Jesus standing in the doorway, inviting me in. I have free will and can refuse to enter. However, if I do step inside, it's as if this particular room was custom designed for me. It may be bare or lie in shambles at the moment, but even then I can sense a potential for something meaningful and good. So I go in, test out my initial impression, and discover that it's for me. God wants me to be there. It's part of his plan for me.

156

Returning to physical therapy was one of the many "rooms" I explored when my daughters entered school. If God does communicate with us through our feelings, thoughts, and desires, I believe the loss of desire for my earlier career came from God. So I closed that door and began seeking other rooms. I didn't know what I wanted. What did God want?

Sometimes an answer to that question just drops into our life. I love it when an opportunity appears by surprise. That happened to me one evening at a friend's house. A few of us were there for a home Mass, celebrated by a priest who was a chaplain at a local hospital. At the end of Mass, he suddenly commissioned each of us to bring communion to Catholic patients at that hospital on Mondays. What? Who, me?

In retrospect, the commissioning was unwise. We had no training for this ministry, but two of us agreed to try it out anyway. Off we went, green as unripe bananas, holding a little handbook that explained how to do a communion service. It did nothing to ease my fear of saying the wrong thing to someone. Before entering each hospital room, I would stand in the hall and fervently pray that the patient on my list wouldn't be there.

It took two Mondays before I tossed aside the handbook because its ritual was far too long for sick people. Years of hospital work heightened my awareness of patient needs and energy levels. A physical therapy background helped me in my new work and showed me something I've often seen since then: *God never wastes anything that's happened to us.*

What has occurred, what we've learned, who we know, where we've been: Our past may have been horrible or splendid or all points in between. Whatever it's been, God's infinite creativity will find amazing ways for it to contribute to a life-giving future for us and for others. Our task: stay close to God and open to possibilities. God's task: lead us. Often the path takes us where we never expected to go.

4. *Personal sense of "rightness."* Here is the essence of Saint Ignatius's step 3 in the discernment process. It's deeper than reasoning but not opposed to it. Instead, to me this step feels like heightened awareness, like a spiritual antenna that's tuned into ideas. I'm open to opportunities and to trying out each one. When an option isn't part of God's plan for me, I tend to feel a certain heaviness within me, a total absence of energy. That gives me a clue that this one isn't for me.

Most opportunities go nowhere, but that's OK. If I get discouraged, I recall America's poster boy for perseverance: Thomas Edison. He had a lot to say on that topic, including, "When you have exhausted all possibilities, remember this: you haven't." So I keep on keeping on, still praying, still trusting that God has something good in mind for me. Eventually a door into the future does open, and I get a sense of rightness about it, a feeling that this one fits me and my current circumstances.

God rarely shows me anything about my long-range future. Nevertheless, when I look back on a decision, I often see the unfolding of a wonderful plan, invisible when I initially said yes, but now as clear as lines on a map.

For example, bringing communion to hospitalized patients awakened in me a desire for more education. That led to my taking a two-year healing ministry training course created by Father Leo Thomas.[2] That led to the two of us coauthoring his legacy. After his death, knowledge I gained from him resulted in two more books, including this one.

Each of these steps began with "yes," but not without questions and qualms on my part. God answered them with great consistency:

- Was I qualified to do this? *Answer*: No. Not at the moment, but eventually, yes. Jesus would be with me the whole time. "Remember, I am with you always, to the end of the age" (Matt 28:20b).

- Would I make mistakes? *Answer*: Yes, many of them, but God was bigger than my errors. Jesus could be Lord of my mistakes and even bring good out of them. "Nothing will be impossible with God" (Luke 1:37).
- Would this ministry cost me something economically, emotionally, and/or physically? *Answer*: Yes. This is the cross of Jesus: "He said to them all, 'If any want to become my followers, let them deny themselves and take up their cross daily and follow me'" (Luke 9:23).

So I wasn't qualified, I would blow it and also, by the way, suffer. If a business listed these items in an ad, responses might fluctuate between zero and one. But for some mysterious reason, I kept on saying yes to God. Then came work and a slow unfolding of his plan, one I never could have imagined.

DECISIONS, DECISIONS

If each decision we made involved the above process, every action would be a big deal. Instead, for daily matters, we use discernment instinctively. What to do today, whether to buy something, where to eat: God has given us common sense and a brain to use for day-to-day living.

For bigger matters, spiritual companions are a great blessing. For major decisions, we may need the help of experts: perhaps a spiritual director with training in discernment methods, or a different professional such as a counselor or physician.

Whether a decision is major or minor, part of the human experience is a lack of absolute certainty about any choice we make. Yes, God's help is there, but it usually isn't very palpable.

This can give rise to loneliness, a feeling that may tempt us to avoid a decision-making moment. Even with the support of others, even after a well thought-out discernment process, the choice ultimately rests with us. Will I or won't I do this? If so, when? How?

Those questions weighed heavily on my mind decades ago when my mother was dying of cancer in Philadelphia while we were here in Seattle. During a prayer time one morning, I sensed that God intended for me to go back east for one last visit—but not yet. God would let me know when.

Thus began weeks and months of waiting. I started to worry. My ever-creative mind imagined getting to Philadelphia too late. At the end of my life, I would arrive at heaven's door and Jesus would say, "You know the few days of prayer times you missed? I tried to tell you then, but you missed it."

I fretted and stewed like that for weeks until one morning the phone rang. On the line was Dad's sister, a delightful woman who happened to be wealthy. "Janet?" she said. "This is your Aunt Janet. I'm calling to tell you that your father's birthday is coming up."

After I assured my aunt that, yes, I was aware of the date, she continued: "The gift I want to give him this year is you and the girls coming here for a visit. If you want to do that, I'll just have my travel agent get in touch with you and send you the tickets for whatever dates you choose. Now if Fred is concerned about my paying for this, you just tell him that I have a nickel."

I can't remember the rest of that call. I do remember my reaction after hanging up: laughter. I think God laughed too: not only did he give me a clue about the timing of my visit, he even sent me the tickets.

The girls and I flew to Philadelphia a few weeks later. Vibrant fall colors, fun times with my siblings, Dad, Aunt Janet, and a final visit with Mom: The timing was perfect, and why wouldn't it be? God had planned it that way.

CONCLUSION

Whether it's the specific timing of a visit like mine or a major life decision, God has plans for each of us—not just one plan, but many big and seemingly little ones that build upon our earlier choices. Our infinitely creative God wants us to know his will. Therefore, he communicates with us through whatever means we're best able to experience him:

- a telephone call,
- a scripture passage,
- a book like this one,
- a spiritual director,
- a spiritual companion,
- a family member,
- a stranger,
- a child,
- a sermon,
- a song,
- a symphony,
- a painting,
- a story,
- a sunrise,
- a sunset,
- and so many more.

God of heaven and earth, thank you for caring about the choices I make. Thank you for leading me toward fullness of life. I ask you to give me ears to hear, eyes to see, and a heart to sense your will for me today, tomorrow, and on into the future. Speak, Lord, your servant is listening. Amen.

FOR YOUR REFLECTION

1. This chapter includes the following scripture from Jeremiah 29:11–13:

   I know the plans I have for you, says the LORD, plans for your welfare and not for harm, to give you a future with hope. Then when you call upon me and come and pray to me, I will hear you. When you search for me, you will find me.

   a. Have you ever had a sense of God having plans for you?
   b. If yes, what were/are those plans?
   c. If no, what are your thoughts or feelings about that fact? Would you like to have some idea about God's plans for you?
2. This chapter looks at two views of God's will: a predetermined road map, or a daily spiritual journey with many choices for reaching abundant life for yourself and others.
   a. Does either of these views match your thinking?
   b. What do you think God's will is for you?
3. Four items need to fit together in order to make wise choices. Recall a time you struggled to decide about an important issue. How many (if any) of the following

came into play during your decision-making process? What was the result?

a. Scripture and the teachings of your church
b. Community input
c. Personal circumstances
d. Personal sense of "rightness"

4. If you have a spiritual companion, what role has this person played when you've been making an important decision? Was he/she helpful? Unhelpful? Not part of the process?

5. God communicates with us through whatever means we're best able to experience him. How does God communicate with you? How are you best able to experience him?

6. For more about this topic, I recommend a book by Father James Martin, SJ, *The Jesuit Guide to (Almost) Everything: A Spirituality for Real Life*. I found chapter 12: "What Should I do?" to be especially helpful. The following is from that chapter:

Every state of life, every decision, includes some pain that must be accepted if you are to enter fully into those decisions, into new life. There is no perfect decision, perfect outcome, or perfect life. Embracing imperfections helps us relax into reality. When we accept that all choices are conditional, limited, and imperfect, our lives become, paradoxically, more satisfying, joyful, and peaceful.[3]

APPENDIX

Affirmations

Chapter 5 looked at the power of affirmation to change people's lives. Here are a few of the many God-given gifts you may see in others—or that others may see in you!

Acceptance	Empathy
Affirmation	Encouragement
Awareness	Endurance
Caring	Enthusiasm
Clarity	Faith
Commitment	Flexibility
Common sense	Friendliness
Compassion	Generosity
Competence	Gentleness
Courage	Graciousness
Creativity	Gratitude
Dedication to God	Helpfulness
Dependability	Honesty
Discernment	Hope

SEEKING *Christ* THROUGH *Friendship*

Hospitality

Humility

Humor

Inner strength

Insight

Integrity

Joy

Kindness

Laughter

Listening

Love

Music

Nurturing

Openness

Patience

Perseverance

Prayer

Reliability

Scripture

Self-discipline

Sensitivity

Servant's heart

Sharing

Sincerity

Tenderness

Thoughtfulness

Touch

Understanding

Warmth

Wisdom

Words

Notes

INTRODUCTION

1. Janet Erskine Stuart, quoted in *Give Us This Day* 5 (October 2015): 238.

2. "I came that they may have life, and have it abundantly" (John 10:10b).

CHAPTER 1

1. Throughout this book, "Meg" is a blend of several spiritual companions. Occasionally I give other names (disguised to protect their identity), in which case I'm speaking of only one person.

2. The importance of community is covered in depth in chapter 5 of *Healing as a Parish Ministry* by Leo Thomas, OP, and me (Seattle: Byron Books, 2000). Originally published by Ave Maria Press (Notre Dame, IN, 1991).

CHAPTER 2

1. Father Leo describes this experience in his and my book, *Healing Ministry: A Practical Guide* (Kansas City: Sheed & Ward, 1994), 219.

SEEKING *Christ* THROUGH *Friendship*

2. James Martin, *Jesus: A Pilgrimage* (New York: HarperCollins, 2014), 199.

CHAPTER 3

1. After Father Jack had received extensive spiritual director training, he mentioned an occasional forehead-slapping memory of mistakes he'd made with me, his first directee. I said I was learning too and, together, we had come through the experience in great shape.

2. Here is how Father James Martin, SJ, has explained the difference between spiritual direction and what he calls "spiritual conversation": "It's different than 'spiritual direction,' where someone helps 'guide' another person in the spiritual life. Here the conversation is between peers, with no one 'directing' other than the Holy Spirit." Quoted in *Give Us This Day* 5 (August 2015): 7

3. "I know the plans I have for you, says the LORD, plans for your welfare and not for harm, to give you a future with hope" (Jer 29:11).

4. More information about Cursillo can be found at www .cursillo.org.

CHAPTER 4

1. My book *Healing: Stories of Faith, Hope, and Love* (Mahwah, NJ: Paulist Press, 2003) includes a chapter on forgiveness of others (chap. 18).

CHAPTER 5

1. Henri Nouwen, *Turn My Mourning into Dancing* (Nashville: Thomas Nelson, 2004), 52–53.

2. Several years ago, Western Washington University conducted an experiment that confirmed students' oblivion to the world around them while on cell phones: A clown on a unicycle pedaled in the campus's main square for an hour. Researchers then asked hundreds of pedestrians if they'd seen anything unusual. Most of the people who were walking alone, listening to music, or walking with friends saw the clown. Cell phone users? Twenty-five percent noticed him. The rest had what they called "inattentional blindness." In the cruise ship story discussed in this chapter, the husband had what could be called "inattentional deafness."

3. Pope Francis, *The Joy of the Gospel* (Erlanger, KY: Dynamic Catholic Institute, 2014), no. 88.

4. M. Scott Peck, *The Road Less Traveled* (New York: Simon and Schuster, 1978), 120–21.

CHAPTER 6

1. Experts put a variety of numbers on exactly how important body language is, but on this they agree: it conveys more than 50 percent of what we say to one another. A commonly cited figure is 55/38/7, meaning 55 percent body language; 38 percent tone of voice; 7 percent actual words. If words convey only 7 percent of meaning, what does this say about the ability of text messaging to build and support close relationships?

2. This speedy tour of Europe marked the beginning of six months of living, studying, and working in Germany. My life-changing sojourn is described in *Quests: Travel Stories of Seeking and Finding* (Seattle: Byron Books, 2014). Available through Amazon.com.

3. Mark Twain, *The Adventures of Tom Sawyer* (New York: Library of America, 1982), 22.

4. Question 4 comes from *Healing Ministry: A Practical Guide*, 179.

CHAPTER 7

1. Together, Father Leo and I wrote two books and a two-year spiritual formation program for an organization called Institute for Christian Ministries (ICM). ICM has unfortunately ceased to exist, but our two books are still available through Amazon.com: *Healing as a Parish Ministry: Mending Body, Mind, and Spirit* (Seattle: Byron Books, 2000) and *Healing Ministry: A Practical Guide* (New York: Sheed & Ward, 2001). My third one is available in e-book format: *Healing: Stories of Faith, Hope, and Love* (Mahwah, NJ: Paulist Press, 2003).

CHAPTER 8

1. Chapters 5 through 11 in *Healing: Stories of Faith, Hope, and Love* cover these types of prayer.

2. These personality types are described in the Myers-Briggs Type Indicator. They divide personality preferences into four categories: Introversion-Extroversion; Sensing-Intuition; Thinking-Feeling; Judging-Perceiving. The relationship of these preferences to prayer is covered in depth in Chester P. Michael and Marie C. Norrisey, *Prayer and Temperament: Different Prayer Forms for Different Personality Types* (Charlottesville, VA: The Open Door, 1991). I highly recommend this book.

3. Elizabeth B. Rooney, "Blind Man's Bluff," in *All Miracle: Packages* (Blue Mounds, WI: Brigham Farm Publishing, 2001), 63. Used with permission.

CHAPTER 9

1. Henry David Thoreau, *Walden* (New York: Library of America, 1985), 430.

2. Praying with a companion is covered in the next chapter.

3. Frederick Buechner, *Now and Then: A Memoir of Vocation* (San Francisco: HarperSanFranciso, 1991).

CHAPTER 10

1. Ron Rolheiser, "Pentecost Happened at a Meeting," *Catholic Northwest Progress*, January 30, 2003.

2. Not only did I feel people's prayers during my recovery from surgery. Those prayers worked. I experienced very little post-op pain and had no complications. I felt well after only three weeks, yet doctors had told me it would take six months for me to feel like myself again. Scientific proof exists for results like this. Here's how I describe it in *Healing: Stories of Faith, Hope, and Love*: "What religious people have known for millennia, medical and scientific communities now confirm through studies. Physician and researcher Dr. Larry Dossey believes that if prayer were a new drug or surgical technique, it would be proclaimed a scientific breakthrough," 35.

CHAPTER 11

1. This information about Saint Francis of Assisi is from Thomas J. Craughwell, *Saints for Every Occasion: 101 of Heaven's Most Powerful Patrons* (Charlotte, NC: C. D. Stampley Enterprises, 2001), 233–38.

CHAPTER 12

1. Ignatian Discernment of Spirits is a huge topic, too large to cover within these pages. Here's one definition: "A process by which we become aware of the movements in our hearts, understand where they come from, and either accept or reject them." Timothy Gallagher, OMV, *The Discernment of Spirits:*

An Ignatian Guide for Everyday Living (New York: Crossroad, 2005), 17.

2. Chapters 2 and 7 in this book describe Father Leo Thomas and my work with him.

3. James Martin, *The Jesuit Guide to (Almost) Everything: A Spirituality for Real Life* (New York: HarperCollins, 2012), 338.